SKETCHES FROM THE KAREN HILLS

BY

ALONZO BUNKER

Edition : Culturea (culurea.fr), 34 Hérault
Contact : infos@culturea.fr
Impression : BOD, Norderstedt (Allemagne)
ISBN : 9791041984749
Date de publication : juillet 2023
Mise en page et maquettage : https://reedsy.com/
Cet ouvrage a été composé avec la police Bauer Bodoni

Sketches From The Karen Hills

I - EXPLORATION OF THE LOIKAW MISSION

In the beginning of the year 1866 the writer, with his wife, landed in Burma for missionary work. He was designated to the Red Karens, or Karenni tribe, then a practically unknown people. Having acquired his missionary knowledge largely from Wayland's "Life of Dr. Judson," he settled down to a life work among the frontier tribes of Burma. Though ultimately changed to the Karens of Toungoo, our first love for the Red Karens was not forgotten. Through long years of labour for the Karen tribes about Toungoo, we never ceased to pray and plan for the good of our first love. So, late in the year 1868, an opportunity arising, Dr. Vinton, of the Rangoon Karen Mission, and myself planned a survey of the Red Karen country. This was the beginning of the work which finally took shape in the Loikaw Mission. The journey was, at the time, regarded as specially hazardous, since it was undertaken among unknown, wild, and savage tribes. The country was also reported to be in the throes of feudal warfare. It was, therefore, with some misgivings that we set out from Shwaygeen, with three elephants and a large company of followers (native pastors and servants), for this unknown land.

Our course for the first few days was directly eastward, toward the Salwen River, through dense forests and jungle, inhabited by wild tribes of Karens. Four days brought us to the town of Papoon, on the Yoonzalen River. Here were the headquarters of the district magistrate, under the English government. We found here, also, a few Karen Christians.

The remaining journey must be pursued through an absolutely unknown country, lying along the Salwen River, and extending hundreds of miles to the north. This region included the Karenni tribes, which we had undertaken to visit. Refitting our expedition at Papoon, we sought guides to conduct us through the country, but without success; for the people were in great fear of the savages, and naturally the most dreadful calamities were predicted, if we should persist in our purpose. For not only was the country unknown and poorly mapped, but it was peopled by numerous tribes of Karens which, although of one common stock, were at constant feudal warfare with one another, and especially suspicious of strangers. However, gathering all possible information of the country, we were able, with the aid of the rough maps we had secured, and some astronomical instruments, to set out hopefully. On the second day we saw signs of war in demolished houses, ruined villages, and obstructed roads. Though we were following a road which in times of peace was travelled by large companies of traders, yet for several days we met no one. A great fear seemed to reign over the whole land.

The third day we found our way obstructed with bamboo spikes, arranged to prevent travellers passing to and fro. These spikes were a cruel weapon, about a foot long, their points hardened in fire, and so planted as to be invisible. One of our bearers was badly injured by them.

Dr. Vinton took careful observations for latitude and longitude daily, and on the fourth day by these aids we reached the banks of the Salwen River in the heart of the disturbed district. Here we found a large village entirely deserted, though the houses were uninjured, and the fruit trees in full bearing. In a kyoung, a priest's house, we found a Shan manuscript in good preservation, which we took with us.

Being in need of supplies, and also for the purpose of exploring the country, we camped on the bank of the Salwen at the mouth of a large brook flowing down from the westward mountains. The same silence and absence of inhabitants marked this delightful spot, and the whole face of the country, though abounding in fruits, wild honey, and a variety of wild animals, appeared to have been deserted for months. We pitched our camp in the strongest possible position, to withstand attacks from probable bands of robbers, and settled down to await our supplies of rice. While waiting, we passed the time in hunting game for food. One day Dr. Vinton and myself separated, circling through the forest, and finally both came down to the main road. As I drew near I heard a shout from my companion: "I have been taken prisoner. Come to my help." But as this was laughingly spoken, I knew the case could not be serious. Coming in sight, I saw him surrounded by a band of as savage-looking men as I ever saw. They had all the marks of freebooters.

Altar for Sacrifice

The Red Karen Village of Kelya

Yet it was very soon manifest to me, however, that Dr. Vinton, instead of being taken prisoner, had taken the whole company captive. His perfect knowledge of the language and of native customs, and his remarkable power of story-telling, with his strong personality, had already woven its spell round them, and we soon had the whole band in camp. Our purpose was not only to keep them from doing harm, but also to learn all we could about the country, and to impress upon them the fact that we were messengers of the living God, seeking only their good. They said, "How can you find your way through this wilderness without guides?" and we pointed to our surveying instruments, which seemed to fill them with awe, and answered, "These are our guides." This greatly increased their surprise, which became overwhelming when we bade them listen to the talking of our large chronometer. After this exhibition, they kept at a respectful distance from these instruments and held frequent discussions in which it became evident by their gestures that it was of these they were talking. That night we assigned them quarters where they could have the least possible advantage over us. But when these wild men joined us, by invitation, at our evening worship, and saw the reverent attitude of our Karen Christians, and listened to their sweet singing, such as they had never heard, and our worship had closed with a petition to the God who cares for His children, the effect upon them was such that we no longer distrusted them.

On the morrow, with our stranger visitors for guides, and with full supplies of food, we set out for the capital of Western Karenni, several days' journey to the north. Our guests, who had become quite companionable, gave us abundant information about our journey and about the state of the country.

As we passed through a deserted village, we found tamarind trees in full fruit. The acid of this fruit is very grateful when travelling. In a moment packs were thrown off, guns leaned against trees, and our followers were in the trees gathering fruit to take with them. This seeming recklessness excited the amazement of our visitors, who said: "You surprise us exceedingly in a place like this, where we dare not travel alone, or lay aside our weapons for a moment; but you people throw them aside as though there were no bad men about, and seem to be entirely without fear." Dr. Vinton improved this incident to impress upon them again the watchful care of the God we served.

Some miles ahead our new friends separated from us, taking the road to the right, which led to Eastern Karenni, while we pursued our way to the left, directly north. The road was now plain before us, and our progress rapid. In two days' travel we began to see signs of the inhabitants of the land and. Tillers of the soil were going to their fields in groups of two and three, all fully armed. We were entering a country where the spirit of evil had supreme sway, as was evident on every hand. At every branching road were altars built to the evil spirits, on which offerings were exposed. Small huts, also, were built on rising knolls to propitiate the spirits of the fields, and to insure good crops. The country was largely cleared, the inhabitants numerous, signs of labour multiplied, and interest increased as we advanced.

We seemed a small force to accomplish our object, and indeed we were merely the forerunners of the Lord's army, advancing to the deliverance of those who had long been under the destroying bondage of Satan; and this conviction filled us with a holy enthusiasm. Messengers had been sent to notify Koontee, the chief ruler of the Western Karenni, of our approach, and about noon on the fourth day we saw a great company of natives grouped on the top of a high hill, up which we were advancing. As we came in sight, we were welcomed by a heavy discharge of native firearms, the beating of tom-toms, and the blare of trumpets.

Koontee was an old man of kindly look, and he extended to us a hearty welcome. He said he had long looked for our coming, that he had heard of the gospel we proclaimed, and that he eagerly desired schools for his people. After a brief conversation, he took the lead toward his chief village, about two miles distant. We were escorted by an immense crowd of noisy natives, who expressed their delight by shouts, mimic warfare, dancing, and other childish manifestations. Reaching his village, we were assigned the deserted house of a carpenter. It was clean and ample for our needs. It was a large village of seven or eight hundred houses, well built, and for the most part cleanly. Here we spent a week preaching and teaching. The old chief, a descendant of a long line of reigning chiefs, was most cordial. He said, "My father loved this way, of which a missionary told him, who spent only a brief time here." [He had reference, doubtless, to Dr. Mason, who made a hasty tour there years before.] He further said, "I wish to have my children acquainted with books." He knew very little of the gospel, but seemed anxious to know more. He was supposed to be the ruler of sixty thousand people, or more.

During our stay, the singing of our band of Karen Christians had a marked effect upon the young people, and several classes were formed for the study of the Karen alphabet, and for learning to sing. One young man, named Ngapah, connected with the reigning family, was so impressed that he resolved to accompany us back to Toungoo to pursue a course of study. He became the first convert to Christ among the Red Karens, and ultimately preached the good news among his own people. He thus proved to be the first fruit of the subsequent Loikaw Mission.

While the early work among the Red Karens was not so fruitful as in some other Karen tribes, yet some rare jewels of Christian devotion were won among the common people. The first of these was Ngapah, just mentioned. The Holy Spirit wrought in him a miracle of grace, producing one of the most conspicuous Christian characters in all the Toungoo Mission. He was a conscientious, faithful, intelligent servant of the Lord Jesus. He had ever the good of his people at heart, and their salvation was the supreme effort of his life. And his labours for them were successful. Doubtless, his name will stand high on the roll of the faithful in the heavenly land.

Our return to Toungoo was directly westward over the successive ranges of intervening mountains, and the journey was full of adventure, spiced with not a little danger. The tribes encountered were semi-hostile, and did what they could to block our way. But by careful watching, both night and day, we broke through opposition and safely reached home.

On the first day of the return trip, as we reached the top of a mountain, on which a large Red Karen village was built, the confusion among the people was so great we at first thought our progress was being opposed. The villagers seemed wild with excitement. The elephants and ponies, and still more the white strangers, seemed to stimulate their curiosity to a wild degree. They rushed upon us, clapped their arms about us, and shouted in their excitement. We soon found, however, that it was only the excitement of curiosity; and when we asked for water and a place to camp, they were full of cordial hospitality. In gathering wood for a fire, Dr. Vinton approached a large tree and began to gather the dead limbs beneath it, when the people rushed upon him with loud exclamations of horror. An explanation showed the tree to be the home of a powerful nat, or evil spirit, who would slay those who approached him. An unusual opportunity was thus given us to teach these people about the mighty God, of whom they now heard for the first time. And as we took all our wood from this tree without receiving personal harm, they seemed convinced of their error. The afternoon was passed in cordial intercourse, and the next day we departed with mutual expressions of esteem. The chief of the village proved this by following us till noon, and by restoring a large knife which one of his subjects had appropriated.

One scene remains fixed in memory as marking the strenuous character of the opposition to our progress. All one day we had been marching, clearing the road as we went, in which work an intelligent elephant bore a large part by removing trees which the natives had felled across the road to impede our march. Drawing near a native village, from which much of the opposition had arisen, we saw the people gathered in apparently hostile array on a hill-top. Our elephant made quick work in clearing out the fallen trees in front, when, having put our caravan in compact form, we marched up the hill in close order. Well do we remember Dr. Vinton leading the caravan, and as we approached the compact mass on the hill-top, he shouted, "Make way, make way, that the children of the mighty God may pass!" As he called out in English, the savages were astonished by the cry, and so gave way, and the three elephants and several ponies with native bearers and servants all filed through in compact array, while the two missionaries stood on either side and guarded them as they passed.

A few more days brought us in safety to Toungoo. This proved to be the opening journey for founding the future mission at Loikaw. On this visit a native missionary by the name of S'Aw was appointed to the Red Karens, and took up his residence at Kelya, the capital of the western province. He was a man of great devotion and faith. His whole family (wife and two children) had been stolen by this people when he was pastor on the Toungoo frontier, some years before. This cruel treatment, however, slackened not his devotion to the Red Karens. For many years he consecrated all his powers to their good and salvation. He would have been a notable worker in any land. It was not until worn out by years of lone service in Kelya that he returned to Toungoo, where he died.

II - EXPLORATION CONTINUED

It should be stated that in those days the village of Loikaw was without importance, but acquired some note when the English government, in settling the Southern Shan States, chose it for a military post, thus making it a post town. It is situated on the northern boundary of the Karenni States, and on a small river running south from Eagle Lake. South of it were the Eastern and Western Karenni States, to the southwest were the Brec tribes, while on the west several minor tribes of Karens were located. Then northwest of Loikaw was the strong and vigorous tribe of Padong Karens, and also the peculiarly peaceable and teachable tribe called the Goung Does. The Shans and Tong-thoos and some other races dwelt on the north. All these combined to form the Loikaw Mission.

Some four years after S'Aw was located as missionary in Western Karenni, a second expedition in the interests of the work was undertaken from Toungoo. It was proposed to cross the mountains from Toungoo directly eastward to Karenni, a distance of ten or twelve days' journey.

This long journey being regarded as hazardous for a single missionary, Rev. Norman Harris, of Shwaygeen, joined the company. He was better known among us younger missionaries as "Father Harris," and to us there was no one in all Burma who better sustained this character. His round face, illumined by the light which comes from strong faith in God, still shines in our memories. With such a counsellor and helper, we felt strong for the journey. We were also strengthened by the presence of S'Aw, the Red Karen missionary, and Ngapah, the first convert from that people.

Early on the 12th of December, 1871, we set out from Toungoo with our little company. The first night we were drenched with rain, and the mountain-sides became so slippery that our progress was very slow. Finally we left our two elephants and got Karen bearers, who took our goods in conical baskets on their backs, this change enabling us to travel more rapidly. On the 21st of December we reached the capital of Western Karenni. The reigning chief was absent, settling political questions among his people.

We were quartered in a large and commodious building, but it was cursed in the eyes of the people, because "its former owner had the power to destroy life by magic." This superstition holds sway among this people, and many are condemned to death only because they are regarded as witches or wizards, able to destroy life. The reader will note that the "Salem witchcraft" has changed its location. The act of quartering us in a place which had been cursed did not promise a cordial reception! The people would naturally be deterred from visiting us until they should see that we remained unharmed. This becoming manifest, they resorted to us in increasing numbers. They also listened with growing respect to our preaching. The children, especially, became interested in the singing of the young men who accompanied us, and we soon had a fine school in our quarters. Some were eagerly studying the "ABC" of the Karen language, and others were learning to sing the Karen hymns. Thus our days were full of work.

At the service held on the first Sunday in this village a large number assembled in the house, but more sat outside; for the fear of the evil spirits had not yet worn off.

Two days before our departure, Koontee, the ruling chief, returned and greeted us with great cordiality. He gave us every encouragement possible to appoint teachers in his village and to establish schools. Also a number of young men and women declared their intention of returning with us to Toungoo to enter the school there. Earnest consultations of the omens by the people, as to the safety of their journey, took place. This consisted in the inspection of the thigh bones of a fowl; which was merely the old superstition of divination as practised by most heathen nations.

On the night of our departure there was much excitement among the young people, opposed in many cases by their elders, in deciding whether they would go to Toungoo, or remain at home. On the 27th of December we arose at midnight to prepare for the homeward journey. It was a beautiful moonlight night, and, as we filed out of the village, we were escorted by the old chief, who exhorted us: "Do not forget my people. They are very ignorant and superstitious. Come again, and bring us the white book." We found that several slaves had followed us. Altogether we had a formidable company of those who had determined to leave their darkness and to seek the true light.

Our journey home was rapid; but the jungle fever prostrated both Father Harris and myself. Climbing a high mountain, myself in the lead, I heard a groan and a fall. Glancing back, I saw Father Harris' great form prostrate, his head down the slope of the mountain-side. He had fainted from his fever.

On the 3rd of January we reached home from one of the most successful missionary tours we ever made. This gave a great impetus to the gospel among the young people of Karenni, and they began to come to our school in groups of two or three in subsequent years. They readily assimilated with other Karens in school duties, and rapidly acquired the Karen dialect taught in the school. Also, on receiving religious instruction, they eagerly embraced the Christian faith, and joined the school church. In a decade and a half, upwards of eighty became followers of our Lord, and many of the young men became devoted and zealous preachers of the gospel. Thus was the work of the coming Loikaw Mission rapidly advancing, though we did not realise the fact.

Several years followed, and a third tour was planned. In this we were joined by Rev. Dr. Rose and his friend, Mr. McCall, from Rangoon. Much knowledge of Karenni had now been gained. In fact, the whole country between the Toungoo Valley and the Salwen River had been opened up to missionary effort. Owing to the peculiarly prepared condition of the Karens for the reception of the gospel, through their established traditions, all this wild territory, with its many Karen tribes, became exceedingly attractive to missionary workers; for most of the tribes readily responded to Christian teaching. Hence this expedition was undertaken with high hopes. A rapid journey across the mountains brought us again to Kelya. We found that great progress had been made among the people. The increase of religious knowledge was apparent everywhere. This was due to the faithful labour of S'Aw and his associates, including the many young men educated in Toungoo, who had returned to their own country.

Koontee, the chief of Western Karenni, had died; but his successor, Koonsaw, was equally cordial. Indeed, he gave strong evidence of having embraced Christ by faith as his Saviour. In proof of his good will, on one occasion he took from his side a silver-mounted sword, one of the tokens of his authority, and gave it to the missionary with an earnest exhortation that he continue the work for the education of his people. This had been enjoined upon him by his father, Koontee, and he had promised to effect all he could in this line.

After spending a delightful week or more in Kelya, we recrossed the watershed towards Toungoo, followed by numbers of young men and women going to Toungoo for study. In the meantime, Ngapah had grown to be a mature Christian, and was most useful in the mission.

We must not omit an interesting incident of this tour. One morning we were entering a pass, toward the top of the highest range, when a strong home feeling came over us. Glancing around, we saw, to our surprise and joy, what we had never seen, save in New England, multitudes of dandelions and both white and blue violets in full bloom. Their bright, laughing eyes filled us with new inspiration and courage for our work. For they seemed to presage the time when all that dark, sin-cursed land would come as fully under the sway of our Redeemer as the most evangelised parts of New England. Nay more, they seemed bright omens of that glorious day when "the kingdoms of this world shall become the Kingdoms of our Lord, and of His Christ; and He shall reign for ever and ever."

The First Converts from the Loikaw Mission

As we climbed the mountains it became very cold, and one morning, emerging from our tent, we found the ground white with frost; and a little further on we broke thin ice from a pool of water. This was a rare treat for the natives, who, living on the plains, had never seen such sights, nor felt the bracing tonic of such atmosphere.

As we neared our destination, we became oppressed with the question as to how we were to meet the expense of supporting the youths who were urgently seeking an education at our Toungoo school. So impressed was Dr. Rose with the importance of this work that he offered to meet the need by gathering funds in Rangoon. This promise he fulfilled, his friends generously responding to his call for help.

From this time onward the work among the border tribes was pursued with all the resources that the mission could command. Repeated tours were made among Padoungs and Northern Karen tribes. The native missionaries were very zealous in their travels, and did good work. As a result, churches were established among the Brecs, the Padoungs, and other tribes.

Twenty-five or thirty miles northwest of Kelya there was founded a flourishing little church at the village of Daushee-I. This was largely accomplished through the instrumentality of one of nature's noblemen, named Tu-Ri, whom God has raised up from the heathen. He was a rare Christian character, of a strong personality, and of large executive ability. He accepted the teachings of Christ with his whole heart, and reserved neither strength nor property in promoting the work in connection with the native missionaries at Daushee-I. The church grew rapidly, a good school was established and maintained, and through the beneficence of Deacon Walter L. Clark, of Providence, R. I., a fine board chapel was erected, which provided a home for the missionaries also, who subsequently occupied the field.

During several subsequent years, much was accomplished by the missionaries in travelling through all the region embraced in the Loikaw field. One season, accompanied by Dr. J. N. Cushing, we travelled with an English company of troops under command of Colonel Sartorious, going through all the Southern Shan States. This tour extended also into Eastern Karenni and other neighbouring States. In this expedition the best of relations were established with the native chiefs, and large missionary interests projected. As the results of this tour, politically, the little village of Loikaw, composed of Shans, Burmans, and Eastern Karennies, was chosen as a military station for the Southern Shan States, thereby largely increasing its influence on the surrounding country.

During these years the knowledge of the gospel had been scattered far and wide throughout these numerous tribes. The results in numbers baptised were comparatively small; but manifestly the whole region was well prepared for a great work of ingathering.

III - FOUNDING OF THE LOIKAW MISSION

In the autumn of 1899, God, in His Providence, seemed to show that the set time had come to establish the Loikaw Mission. We give a brief résumé of the conditions in the Toungoo hills, pointing to this event. Eastward from Toungoo City, the gospel of the Lord Jesus had been diligently proclaimed throughout English territory back to the watershed range between Toungoo Valley and the Salwen River. It had overflowed this boundary into the savage Brec country, and conquered this wild tribe. The evangelist had passed around to the south of this country earlier in its history, had entered Western Karenni, and had wrought a great revolution in the sentiment of the people towards Christianity. Native workers had been stationed in Eastern Karenni, a State larger than the Western, and good had been wrought. Loikaw was on the extreme northern limit of this State. The gospel also had been proclaimed from Toungoo City north and northeastward to the boundary of the English territory in both directions. Four days' journey northeast from Toungoo was our Christian stronghold in that direction. Having captured Yahdo, as elsewhere narrated, the gospel forces fell upon Senite, in the Padoung country, and captured it for our Lord. True to its genius, the gospel spread to the region around Senite, and crystallised in a large village, on the way to Karenni, under a faithful evangelist named Asoung, which later developed into a large and thrifty church.

The route passing through Senite and the Padoung country proved the most available one to Karenni. The evangelists were accustomed to take this to and from that country, preaching as they travelled.

A strong man, Tu-Ri (before mentioned), moved from Yahdo to a village on the corners of three Southern Shan States, two of them being the Red Karen and Padoung States. This village, Daushee-I, was thirteen miles southwest from Loikaw.

In the autumn of 1899, while the writer was on furlough in America, three letters from as many individuals, written at about the same time, but quite independent each of the other, were received in Boston. These letters were of the utmost importance, in that they urged a speedy appointment of a responsible missionary for this region. They represented the thirst for Christian education as having grown to such an extent among the Eastern Karens that many had determined to secure this from any who would give it to them. Their first choice was teachers from the Society which had been ministering to them. Hence their appeal to the American Baptist Missionary Union for a permanent teacher. If the Missionary Union would send this help, they were content. Otherwise they would apply to other missionary bodies. This meant the Ritualists, with all their evils.

To this appeal the reply of the Missionary Union was that, if the writer would return to Burma and take up this work, the Society would support him. Rev. Truman Johnson, M.D., who had already proved himself a true reproduction of Luke, "the beloved physician," in a long term of service in the Toungoo Mission, was at home on furlough at this time. It was suggested that he might be willing to join the new mission. This he was quick to do, at the request of the Society. The Secretaries at the rooms in Boston pronounced this an "ideal arrangement."

About the first of the year 1900, we gathered our supplies, and, on reaching Burma, set out on the long journey over the Shan Mountains for Loikaw, following the Burma Railway from Toungoo to Thazi, a hundred miles or more. At Thazi we shipped our goods in carts to be taken across the mountains over the great government road, then in process of construction. This was the only route by which goods could be taken to Loikaw, yet it took us a long way to the north of our destination. Crossing the Shan Mountains, we entered upon the great Shan Plateau, where we turned south to Fort Stedman, on the beautiful Ingle Lake. Here we took boats down the Loikaw River, which flowed south from Ingle Lake. The whole journey consumed about thirteen days.

We reached Loikaw the morning of January 17, 1900. The prospect from the first was depressing. A strong wind from the south blew clouds of dust over the village, which we found to be largely composed of Shans, Burmans, and East Indians. Hardly a shade-tree relieved the dull landscape. Our goods were hustled on shore by our boatmen, and we sat down on our boxes, wondering what we should next do. We were completely surrounded by an unsympathetic, if not a hostile, crowd. But the God of missions did not keep us long in suspense; for, as we sat planning our next move, we saw nine strong young men rapidly approaching us, whom we soon recognised as belonging to the Yahdo church over the mountains. Without appointment of any kind, or a knowledge of our coming, except by rumour, they appeared just at the time most needed. This seemed to us a special act of Providence in our behalf, and so we took courage. We found, on enquiry, that there was a Karen clerk in the government house who was a Christian from Bassein. On application to him we were cordially welcomed into his house. Our nine Yahdo volunteers soon had our goods safely piled under his house. Thus at rest for a time, we gave ourselves to earnest prayer for Divine guidance in what we had long felt to be an important step for the spread of the Kingdom of God in that part of Burma. While engaged in prayer, Tu-Ri, the disciple of Daushee-I, appeared with smiling face, leading a large body of his followers from that village for whatever help they could render us.

On looking about Loikaw, we saw nothing to recommend it as a central missionary station, save that it had been made a postal town. We also found that strong opposition to the founding of the mission had been organised, led by the only European government official in the place, and an autocrat in his position. He possessed supreme power as a local officer. The chiefs of the Southern Shan States, though nominally independent, were completely under his control, through fear of his power over them. We found that, though they had been friendly to us for years, and had united in the call for our coming, they were now silenced through dread of this English officer. Moreover, a Roman Catholic Society, that had everything to gain, as they thought, by keeping us out of the country, had a large and strange influence over this officer. He had the power of bestowing or withholding favour. He could hinder us from securing land for mission purposes from the tribal governors. Just here Tu-Ri came forward with the offer of land and other help to establish our mission near his village. He had no fear of the English political officer. We ought to say here that this opposition on the part of an official was exceptional. We have great pleasure in testifying to the uniform courtesy and helpfulness of the English officials in Burma during thirty years' experience. This helpfulness was exemplified in the Lieutenant-Governor's orders in the present case, as related further on.

In consultation with Tu-Ri, the question as to our headquarters was narrowed to three stations–Loikaw, Nwe Doung, about eight miles below Loikaw, both being situated on the east side of the Karenni Valley, and the little village of Daushee-I. Under the escort of Tu-Ri and his followers, after three days' study of Loikaw as a situation, we set out for Nwe Doung. Here we were received in the most friendly manner, but could find no healthful place for a mission dwelling. We then crossed the valley to Daushee-I. Here we found conditions most favourable for our purpose; as we would be located on the corners of three Southern Shan States, and be central for all our work.

Mission House, Loikaw

We left Toungoo with a large purpose in mind, feeling we were to plan a work for many years, and for a large population, consisting of many tribes, who spoke different dialects. With this purpose in view, we set about the study of our present situation with much prayer for Divine guidance. Our good doctor pronounced in favour of the western side of the valley, on grounds of health. The wind in the rainy season blew down from the mountain ranges, making the air pure and comparatively free from malaria. It was also on the direct route to Toungoo, and only four days distant from Yahdo, the halfway station to that city. Moreover, it was in the midst of the population whom we hoped to win to Christ. Villages of the Padoung tribe, Eastern and Western Karenni, and the Brec nations were near at hand, or within easy access at any season of the year. Other considerations added their weight in influencing our decision. The most powerful were the clear leading of Providence. For years previous to our advent, the little church had been organised and more recently a fine large chapel had been erected, Deacon W.L.Clark, of the Broadway Church, Providence, R. I., meeting most of the expense. This would provide temporary quarters for us while erecting a permanent dwelling. The ease with which supplies could be brought from Toungoo for our schools and for our support also had much weight; for the Loikaw Plain became a bog during the rains, and very difficult of passage. The natives offering large help, both in money and labour, also had weight, for the financial support of the mission from home was yet small. Said Dr. Johnson, as we sat overlooking the proposed site, "It truly looks as though the Holy Spirit had directed us to this spot."

After further careful and prayerful consideration of the whole matter, which involved grave interests, we settled on the hill above Daushee-I, which had been given us for this purpose, as the future site of the Loikaw Mission. We retained the name Loikaw, as it was a postal town.

The opposition of the British political officer to our settlement in the Southern Shan States, beginning with our arrival, increased in violence from week to week. He used all resources at his command to defeat our plans, to prejudice the natives against us, forbidding them to receive us and to grant lands for necessary buildings. The Karenni chiefs, who were particularly favourable to us, and who had joined in the appeal for our coming, were obliged to visit us secretly. His opposition culminated by inflicting fines upon those chiefs who had helped us, and ultimately by issuing a government paper, over his own official signature, ordering us to cease building and to withdraw from the land.

But the hand of God was again revealed in our behalf. For the very small mail brought a telegram from the chief officer of the English Government, in Burma, giving us permission to build wherever we might choose, and also ordering this political officer to cease his persecutions of the chiefs, because of help bestowed upon us. And he further ordered him to help us build our station. This stopped all open hindrance; yet this officer kept up secret opposition during the following months. This was specially shown against the native adherents of the mission. Yet our work went forward successfully and rapidly: the efforts of past years forming a good beginning for this new advance. The native evangelists were enthusiastic, and the people far and wide were cordial and ready to help, promising thatch for our new houses. Men brought the grass on the backs of oxen from long distances, while the women gathered to weave it into thatch for house-roofing. The men also helped in carrying timber, and in such other work as their time would allow. We brought sawed teak timber from Loikaw on carts, and also felled trees in the near forests, sawing them up by hand, thus securing lumber for our dormitory and dwelling-house. The necessary hardware and windows we brought from Rangoon on our trip up to Loikaw. In one hundred and forty-nine days we were able to move from the chapel into our mission house. This speedy result was made possibly by the fine business capacity and architectural skill of Dr. Johnson, who pushed the work vigorously against seemingly overwhelming obstacles.

Vegetable gardens were laid out, fenced, and planted with seeds brought from America. In like manner flower gardens were planted, thus providing in anticipation edibles and flowers which would remind us of our dear New England, or present a homelikeness to cheer us in lonely hours. Then the cocoanut palm stood side by side with pines from the hills; pyramids of nasturtiums stood in the front yard, blessing us with their rich colours and perfume; fruits from our garden rested upon our table, and our material circumstances were all we could wish.

One of the strongest elements in the success of the mission was the medical work of the "beloved physician." His hospital at first consisted of a deal box and a chair in the shadow of the Daushee-I chapel. Patients resorted to him from all parts of the country, some with horrible sicknesses, which he treated with the utmost patience and skill. With a suitable building and proper appliances, how much could this element of power have been increased. These materialised in due time, adding a mighty impulse to our work.

Our spiritual work in like manner advanced with encouraging rapidity. The good will of the people, and the long years of Christian instruction they had received made them very susceptible to the influence of the gospel. The little discouraged church of twelve members at Daushee-I sprang into new life. There were fifty present at our first service in the Clark chapel, not including children. This attendance was maintained, and increased gradually. A Sunday school was organised at once, and also a day school. The whole atmosphere of the mission was one of joyous activity. The young people often broke out into song when about their work, and our hearts sang with them in joy and Thanksgiving. Applications for teachers came to us from every quarter, which we supplied as rapidly as possible, until twenty villages were occupied. The results in 1903 were nineteen stations and churches in a population of between three thousand and four thousand. We had twenty-two preachers and teachers at work. In that year there were sixteen baptisms and one hundred and twelve church members. Two hundred and twenty-four were gathered in the schools, and the contributions of the natives for the year were over eight hundred and eighty rupees, or two hundred and ninety-four dollars. These results amply justified our expectations of a richer and more abundant harvest in the near future.

At one time, in discussing ways and means with an officer of the Missionary Union, when the rapid successes gained in this mission were urged as a reason for a more generous support, he exclaimed, "Yes, but we did not expect this interest to assume so quickly the size and importance of an established mission."

It was also feared by some friends of the mission that too large sums of money had been expended upon it to produce such results. But a careful comparison of the amounts expended on several old missions, and also for the founding and support of six new missions in Burma for five years, beginning with 1899, shows that, per convert, much less sums had been expended on the Loikaw Mission during these years.

Every condition seemed to promise abundant future harvests. Several had applied for baptism from Kelya–the old station among the Red Karens which S'Aw had so long occupied; and notes of "harvest home" were heard from every quarter, when the writer's health broke down in May of the second year of the founding of the mission, and he was forced to retire permanently from the mission field. Every plant which God plants must flourish and bear fruit, and to Him be all the glory.

IV - THE FIRST CHRISTMAS IN LOIKAW MISSION

A faded list before us brings vividly to mind one of the pleasantest incidents of our whole missionary life. It was the day before Christmas. Dr. Truman Johnson and I had been working for nearly a year to establish the Loikaw Mission. We had encountered and overcome, by God's manifest help, great difficulties in this work. The site for the mission station was on that of an ancient city, and the streets, garden walls, and fruit trees were left. Our buildings were nearly completed, our mission school had begun its work of enlightenment, and many patients were coming to the hospital daily. Our vegetable and flower gardens were flourishing, reviving pleasant memories of home. Two mounds of nasturtiums in the flower garden were a blaze of colour, and a variety of home plants were likewise in bloom. The Loikaw Mission was in full operation, sending its rays of gospel light into the surrounding gloom of heathenism.

On the eve before Christmas, wearied by the labours of the day, I sat among the flowers, enjoying the cool of the evening. The environment vividly suggested the homeland with its Christmas festivities. The strain of past months of labour and care for the moment rolled away, and pleasing home thoughts, whispered by the surrounding flowers, took their place. Half-regretfully I thought of our isolation in the far-away mountains of Loikaw. No Christmas with home friends for us. Ah, how little could I realise the wonderful and glad surprise the God of missions was preparing for us!

We were many days' travel over high ranges of mountains, among the heathen Hill people. There was no settled transportation over these mountains, and our nearest post-office was thirteen miles distant. These facts shut off any hope of partaking in the home life of Christmas; and with a feeling bordering on depression, as the shadows deepened, I retired to my room, lighted my lamp, and sat down to read. At about eight o'clock the people returned from their evening worship. Hearing their excited voices in the room below, I began to realise that something unusual had occurred, and soon a Karen burst into my room, exclaiming, "Teacher, Moung Lay has returned, and has found your cases of goods from Rangoon, and there is also a box for you from America." Months before we had sent to Rangoon for supplies, and, owing to the long delay, we thought them lost, and had sent Moung Lay to look them up. He had been absent a week,–but that box from America–what could it be? Oh, probably Mr. Phinney, of the Mission Press, had used an American box in which to pack our supplies. "Yes, teacher, we are sure the box is from America, and for you. We know from the marks on it." "Well, bring it up, and let us see what it is." Sure enough, it was a box from home. In a few moments several Karens brought in another, a larger one, and the room was soon filled with heathen and Christian natives, all filled with curiosity to see what had come to their teachers from the fabulous land of plenty. Dr. Johnson, the beloved physician, also joined us, and we soon had the smaller box opened; and out of it sprang Santa Claus with as hearty a "Merry Christmas" as ever was uttered in a Christian land. It was spoken by so many loving friends in package after package. "Why, doctor, it is full of Christmas presents, and to-morrow is Christmas Day. Here's a package for you right on top."

Then the wonderful thing our God had done began to be realised by us. Only One with omniscient power could have so timed the arrival of the boxes that, after fourteen thousand miles' travel, and months in carts and boats, over mountains and across lakes, subject to all the vicissitudes of uncertainty, those precious boxes should be placed before us in this far-away corner of the earth, exactly on the night before Christmas, for which they were intended by the dear givers in the homeland! It was almost past belief. Yet there they were before us, and the natives all about, wild with delight as they saw the beautiful things unrolled before their eyes. A sacred light fell upon these gifts. They seemed to be from heaven, rather than from America. They were certainly God-given, as they were God-inspired. Surely, no one could have thought us weak, had they seen tears fall upon these tokens of friendship. Package after package, now one for the beloved physician, and then one for me, all so clean, so neatly folded and tied. The very strings and wrappings were of interest. Books, pictures framed and unframed, towels and soap, napkins, beautiful vases for flowers, and candy, which made the natives smack their lips with delight. The list before me covers a full sheet of foolscap paper. With special joy we noticed how many of the gifts could be profitably used in our mission work. How could the donors conceive so well just what we needed?

Here were books enough to make the beginning of a mission library. We saw that our dear native Christians, so poor and needy, who had never seen anything so beautiful as the wonderful things coming out of those boxes, could share largely with us in our precious gifts. How rapidly were they learning the object-lesson of Christian love in their experiences of that evening.

The Mary Love Chapel

By midnight the floor, chairs, bed–everything was covered with a Christmas glory. Under a hallowed spell of God's loving care we slept, only to awake to a new surprise in the morning; for the largest of the three cases greeted us as we came from our rooms. In this was the wonderful Christmas cake from a church in New York. It had travelled its long journey without a break, so carefully was it packed. Its large, brown face, with the motto across its forehead, smiled at us a Merry Christmas of its own. Again we reviewed our gifts before a great crowd of natives. Again we took note of how for many days the native Christians could be blessed with this surplus of gifts; for there were many things among them which met their needs, as if the donors had distinctly foreseen them. In fact, in the days following, it was pleasing to see the efforts at clean faces and hands, and the unsnarling of tangled hair, never before acquainted with comb or brush. Company after company came from distant villages to see this strange and unheard-of exhibition. What new views of Christian fellowship were awakened in the minds and hearts of these native Christians, as they listened with open mouth to the story of the gifts, together with the love of the givers for Christ's work among the heathen. Especially did the timing of the arrival of the gifts, by the guiding hand of Providence, appeal to them and draw them towards a God so mindful of His children's happiness.

But this list of the donors–as I scan it today, it awakens in my heart the most hallowed memories. Here are friends who have been helpers in our mission work for thirty years and more. Some of them have finished their work and have gone to their reward; some have ripened in age and yet dwell in the Beulah land, waiting the passage of the river; while others are in the prime of their usefulness. Dear brothers and sisters, do you think your missionaries can ever forget the years of help in loving gifts and helpful messages received by them through all these years? Much less, can God forget? Here their names are all recorded. They are from all over New England, and the Middle and Western States. Even the capital city of the nation has sent its token of interest.

But we must not fail to notice the sweet and cheering messages enclosed in almost every package and book. There was never a sweeter exhibition of love and loyalty to Jesus than these contained–love for His cause everywhere, and specially for the lost heathen. How gladly we regarded it as an offering to our adorable Lord, and thankfully did we ascribe to Him the glory and praise.

While we read over again with quickened heart-beats this now sacred list, our mind turns instinctively toward that devoted worker whom God used in this exhibition of his loving care. Her loyal heart, under God's direction, we believe, inspired this gracious act. Her hands packed those three cases so closely that not a thing was broken. She it was who sent them on their way, timed to reach us to the day and almost the hour. May our Father bless her, and all who shared in this glad Christmas in Loikaw, as do we and scores of native Christians.

Such was the first Christmas celebration ever held in the Loikaw Mission of Burma. May this evidence of God's love be repeated in this mission many times to His own glory.

V - STORIES OF KAREN CHILD-LIFE

When, puffed up by the pride of race, we begin to think ourselves far above the less favoured, we need to be reminded of the fact that God "hath made of one blood all nations of men for to dwell on all the face of the earth," and that differences of race often result from environment. If the mental and moral characteristics of the uncivilised exhibit a wide variety, it should not be forgotten that the highest civilisation has not obliterated similar varieties. Facts show that the white nations by no means monopolise the gifts of God's grace. Each nationality contributes some excellences of its own to the ultimate typical man. The term heathen is a misnomer. In the thought of the more intelligent natives of the East, where the gospel of Christ has been proclaimed, mankind is composed of only two classes–heathen and Christian, the former rejecting Christ and His gospel, while the latter humbly accept both.

Having occasion to cross the Shan plateau, where the gospel had never been preached, we reached a village made up of Shans, Burmans, and Karens. There was a deserted kyoung (rest-house) near the bank of the stream up which we were going, and, being weary, I sat on its steps. It was early morning, and the scene before me reminded me of New England. The grass-plot gently sloped toward the stream of clear, sparkling water, flowing from a lake whither we were going. The kyoung was in the foreground and the village extended backward up the slope. It was like the usual native villages, with many dilapidated bamboo houses. On the right was a wretched hovel of the usual style, of two stories, where the native children had gathered for play. The upper story had a veranda around it, which was reached by a bamboo ladder. As I sat listlessly watching the children, being very ill, a large dog began to bark at me. Directly one of the children, a little girl of eight or ten years, came down the ladder, picked up a stick, and drove the dog away. She was a heathen girl, absolutely ignorant of the God we worship. I acknowledged her service with a bow. She seemed pleased, ran up the ladder, and again joined her companions in their sports.

As my attention had been drawn to her by her kind act, I continued watching the sports of the children with renewed interest. She seemed a bit restless and frequently came to the edge of the veranda to look at the stranger. Soon she took her younger sister by the hand, came down the ladder, and slowly approached me. This act specially impressed me. I was a stranger from a race she had seldom met, if ever, and it was inspiring to note her fearlessness. As she drew near, I thanked her in her own language for driving away the dog. I also took from my pocket a small Burman coin, and gave it to her. And lest her little sister should feel offended, that being my only coin, I have her a banana. These slight presents filled them with joy. Turning about, they held them up for the inspection, as I supposed, of their mother; and immediately the whole village ran together about me. I entered into conversation with the elders. "Have you any schools? Have you any teachers? Does a Buddhist priest live in your village?" To all these questions they replied in the negative. When I asked them if they knew anything of the great God, who created the heavens and the earth, again a negative answer was given. And then they asked: "Who is He? Where does He live?" And as I tried to tell them of His love, and the coming of His Son, they plied me with questions which my limited knowledge of their language left me unable to answer satisfactorily.

Meanwhile, I had cultivated the acquaintance of my two young friends, who seemed to have assumed the proprietorship of the stranger, about whom they hung. In my efforts to explain the great question of God and His Son, I took out my watch, which excited much surprise among them. One, on listening to its ticking, looked up with wide-eyed amazement, and asked in bated breath, "Is this your God?" Unclasping the chain, I handed it to my little friend. An American child, most likely, would have reached out her hand for the treasure, and would have taken it, perhaps, with a "Thank you." Not so this little heathen girl. She stepped back, bowed very low, as an act of homage, and opened her little hand before me, signifying by the gesture that I might place the watch upon her open palm. Apparently, in her view, it would be impolite to take the watch directly from my hand. Her pleasure on receiving the watch was very marked, and her people crowded about her to inspect it and to listen to its "talk." She would not allow it to pass from her hands, but readily exhibited her treasure for inspection. In a few moments she returned the watch, in the act holding it in her clasped hands and touching her forehead with them, another sign of homage, after which she bowed low and opened her hands for me to take the watch. It was all so neatly and gracefully done as to quite win my heart, and to awaken the wish that such heathen customs might be introduced among children of my own land.

We continued our conversation with the villagers, who were polite and respectful, still noticing the two little girls, who kept hovering about us. Soon the older one came near and sat at my feet, looking up into my face to see if I approved her act. This surprised me, but her next move was more surprising; for she arose and seated herself at my side before all the people. This was as strange a thing to do, in the mind of the people, as it was for Queen Esther to enter into the presence of King Ahasuerus. The people looked on with alarm, as if expecting my anger at such boldness. I recognised her confidence by putting my arm around her and drawing her to my side, thus making a place for her sister, which she took. The whole company of villagers seemed immensely pleased with this treatment of the children. Now consider that there was not a Christian among them, nor any one who had probably ever heard of Jehovah until I had proclaimed Him in their hearing; yet their fellowship and approval were most marked; and directly, as my boat and followers came up the river to the landing, they further manifested their fellowship by following me to the boat, and by smiling upon me as I embarked. It was a covered boat, and after waving them a farewell, I withdrew from their sight, involved in deep thought.

This pleasing experience had shown me the heart of the heathen. Somehow a refinement had grown up among them. These little children showed this refinement in their training. By nature they were as beautiful as any children I ever saw. They were clean and well dressed, their hair was neatly arranged, and they showed a gentleness in movement and speech which was winsome. There was life and light in every action, and yet they knew not even the name of the Lord of life and light. Glancing over this company, it was easy to mark the dividing-line between the innocence of childhood and the spiritual blindness of the adults. And this thought suggests the condition of the densely populated East, with its multitudes of children, as engaging and interesting as these, lacking only a knowledge of the Lord of glory to insure the transfer of their loveliness to old age, and so to fit them for the heavenly land.

My boatmen pushed on up the river, and, as we were about to make a turn which would shut my new friends from view, I glanced back for a final sight of them. The villagers were slowly filing away from the river's bank, but my two little friends had followed after my boat a short distance, and soon they passed from sight. I know not whether any missionary has since reached them, or they ever again heard the blessed name of Jesus, the lover of children. Seeing before them the awful future of a heathen education and life, I said to myself: "Can it be possible that so many children in this land, so engaging, so graceful, so easily won as these, must continue to grow up, pass under the dense cloud of ignorance and superstition, and be lost forever?" And many times since have I prayed that God would move His stewards in Christian lands to such liberality in the support of foreign missions that these millions of heathen children may not be left to perish in their spiritual night.

One of the best ways to learn the inner life of any people is by the study of their children. They are usually a reproduction of their parents–little men and women. This is as true among wild peoples as among the civilised. Journeying over the great military road, constructed across the Shan country by the government of Burma, we had an instructive adventure illustrating the above fact. Riding a bicycle, I had left the carts on the road, and had reached a little settlement about noon. Here I awaited the arrival of our company. This settlement represented a group of poor pigstys. A clump of large bamboos offered an attractive shade. I had no sooner thrown myself down for a little rest, than some dozen or more children swarmed around me. They were unusually dirty, yet attractive. Most of them were from six to ten years of age. Few wore any clothes, while the rest had merely an apology for rags. After looking me over, they continued their play. In course of time my followers came up, and, spreading my tent, I settled myself for a good rest, while dinner was preparing. Getting out my last magazines, the little folks, with whom I had become quite well acquainted, were keenly interested in all I did and had. The pictures in the advertising pages particularly attracted them. Though they had probably never seen a book, they were able to distinguish not a few of the pictures, especially those of animals; and I found their remarks more entertaining than the stories in the magazines.

School Children

A Karen Village in the Hills

In my study of these little folks, I noted that one, a dirty girl of about eleven years, clothed in rags, the merest apology for covering, seemed to be the leading character in all their plays. A happy inspiration led me to propose, a feast for them. So calling this girl, and announcing my purpose, she was directed to take the food, prepare the table, and see that each one behaved properly at the feast. This greatly pleased her, and her bright eyes twinkled; for really, had she been washed and clothed, she would have been a remarkably attractive child. Taking a large plate and placing it on a paper upon the ground, I poured on it a cup of white sugar, first giving the hostess a taste, so she might know it was not salt. Then I turned over matters to the hostess. A comical scene ensued. Like a born leader, she marshalled her little companions about the table, and gave them their orders. They were to seat themselves with their right side to the plate, and to eat with the right hand. They were not to talk, and must eat slowly and a little at a time. These directions were carefully obeyed. The combination of rags and tatters and good manners, and the dignity of the hostess, were very amusing.

While meditating on the discovery of so rare a jewel among a bunch of rags and dirt, my reveries were suddenly interrupted by seeing my little lady grasp a handful of sugar and, like a humming-bird, dart away among the huts. But this puzzling act was explained by her immediate return, followed by her mother. Apparently, she could not fully enjoy the feast without her mother sharing it with her. Here was an instance of unselfish child-love not always met in Christian lands.

It is interesting to note how closely children of all races resemble each other. In all their social relations heathen children do not differ from those born in Christian lands. It is only as they begin to think and plan for themselves that they learn the ways of their elders, or diverge from the common innocence of childhood to the adoption of heathen superstitions and practices.

This unity of childhood marks the unity of the human race, and the saying that "human nature is the same in all the world" gains new emphasis when studied from the standpoint of the child. Accordingly, the missionary finds at this point of his new work that he is dealing with familiar problems. These characteristics, which mark the unity of childhood among all races, sometimes appear to be accentuated among less intelligent peoples; so that, before the fogs of sin and ignorance have blurred the image of God in which they were created, they show a strength and brightness more marked than in their more favoured brothers and sisters in enlightened lands. This fact has not received due attention in ethnological studies.

On our first tour of exploration to Karenni, before narrated, we met a case in point which was instructive. In our company were a number of schoolboys, who were sweet singers and otherwise bright pupils in our Toungoo school. In their association with Red Karen children, they quickly formed acquaintances and proved themselves to be good missionaries. The children they were visiting had never seen the white book, nor heard intelligent singing. Our boys soon had a class in the Karen alphabet and in singing. With surprising quickness they learned both the songs and alphabet. Our youthful teachers were in great demand, and enthusiasm ran high. Among others, a young girl perhaps of fourteen years, was quite carried away with the idea of learning to read the white book. In their conferences their relation to the Living God was explained, and Naw De-moo, the little girl referred to, was fired with the desire to learn more of this wonderful Being.

The question of Naw De-moo returning with us to Toungoo for study arose, and was carefully discussed. She would be the only female in the party, and the journey would require ten or twelve days, and be over high ranges of mountains and through forests abounding in wild beasts. As De-moo expressed her desire strongly and repeatedly, the proposition took form. That she might be fully prepared for the hard journey, the difficulties of the way were carefully set before her. One Red Karen boy was to return with us, so that communication would be easy. As she stood before us, she appeared much excited. The difficulties of the journey were again explained. But she was told that, on reaching Toungoo, she would be heartily welcomed by the missionary women, and that we would provide all her needs while engaged in study. Then she could learn to worship the Living God to her fullest satisfaction.

It was a scene long to be remembered. This little child was contemplating the long and dangerous journey to a distant land, where none of her people dwelt, to learn the mysteries of the white book, and of the worship of a new-found God. Her excitement was intense. As she stood before us trembling, we said to her: "De-moo, think well of what you are doing. Make up your mind firmly. If you decide to go with us, well. We will care for you as for an own child." She still hesitated; but, summoning a strength and determination altogether beyond our accepted ideas of heathen children, she exclaimed, "I will go and learn to worship the Living God, live or die."

She was told to prepare herself for the journey, as we would leave early in the morning. As our company filed out from the village the next day, she appeared among us with a small basket of food and clothes held by a strap against her forehead, ready for the journey. A number of her friends also were escorting her. Not once during the long journey did she exhibit signs of homesickness, but patiently tramped along with the caravan, up and down the mountains, and across rivers, until she reached the city of Toungoo. On the way, our Karen boys and the whole company treated her with the utmost politeness, even as though she had been the queen of the Karens. At even-time they made a little booth for her lodging-place, and eagerly helped her as beset they could through every difficulty.

Never have we seen a better exhibition of kindly feeling among civilised races than was shown toward De-moo on this her triumphant journey from darkness to light, from the city of destruction to the city of life. She reached Toungoo in safety, and was most cordially received into the school, as the first Red Karen girl who had dared to make such a long journey in search of a nobler life. She acquired the Sgaw Karen dialect with remarkable quickness. In about a year from her entrance into the school she applied for baptism, and subsequently she married a native Karen pastor, with whom she led a life of remarkable usefulness till the day of her death. Few white children would have shown such courage, faith, and patience in pursuit of a better life. She was, indeed, one of the choice fruits of the Holy Spirit.

Many instances arise in missionary experience to show that God exercises His providential care over heathen children as well as over those of Christian birth. The following incident is given to illustrate this fact. In a village perched on a mountain-side far away in the jungle, a teacher had begun his work of preaching the gospel. Down the mountain-side was a spring which supplied the village with water. According to the usual custom, the young children collected the wood and brought the water for family use. One of the elders of the village had discovered tracks of some wild animals around this spring, and, with visions of a venison dinner, he had planted bamboo spikes about it. This act was called "do-mer" (spike-planting). The spikes were made of the toughest part of the bamboo, were about four feet long, the points sharpened and made hard in fire, and made a very formidable weapon for attack or defence. One morning Naw Paw-Gay, five or six years old, took her bamboo for water. It was longer than herself. She put the strap across her forehead and trotted down the hill to get water for the morning rice. As she stooped to dip the bamboo into the spring, a dark shadow fell upon her and a rushing sound passed over her. Instantly she awoke to her peril, as, looking up, she saw a frightful beast. It was a man-eating tiger which had secreted itself in the grass near the spring to watch for its breakfast. The moment the little girl stooped to dip up the water, the tiger sprang for her head. Missing it, he went over her and fell upon the spikes and was securely impaled upon them. Her terrified screams quickly brought the villagers to her rescue, and they shortly despatched the tiger. Henceforth, the name of Naw Paw-Gay was changed to Ke-Rou-po, or "the tiger-child." The sceptic may call this an accident; but the believer in God's loving care will regard it as a special interposition of Providence.

VI - K'SURDO

"K'SURDO"–this word has been a song of joy to many missionaries during the last half of the nineteenth century. It is a lone mountain about twenty miles southeast from Toungoo City. It is oblong, and rises fifteen hundred feet from the plain on the eastern bank of the Toungoo River. It is so situated as to catch the dry-season winds from both north and south. Throughout the hot season the temperature at the mountaintop is from ten to fifteen degrees lower than on the plains. This affords great relief from the oppressive heat that elsewhere prevails. The mountain was a fortunate discovery for the foreign whites who reside in this part of Burma.

A small Karen village had sought the cool shade of K'surdo, and a conference of churches was appointed to meet there. This drew the attention of the missionaries to the great change of climate between its summit and the plains; and further exploration of the mountain settled the question of K'surdo as a possible sanitarium for the mission.

The mountain's surface is much broken. Deep ravines, starting from the summit, cut its sides in every direction. These ravines are filled with a growth of rattan, numerous dwarf palms, arums, and other tropical plants of richly coloured foliage, which afford constant surprises and pleasure to the lover of nature. The mountain is also covered with large boulders, as though some giant iceberg in past ages had stranded here and dumped its load of rocks. In some places granite boulders of immense size are piled upon each other. These groups of rocks were a constant source of interests, and some of them were named to distinguish them from each other. Prominent among these was the "Treasure-rock," composed of several huge granite blocks, forming a sort of cave, and out of the centre grew a large jack-fruit tree. Native tradition here located the valuables of an ancient village, whose inhabitants were driven away by their enemies. There was also the "Table-rock," a level shelf of the mountain, which afforded a charming place for picnics, as it was densely shaded by bamboos and creepers. The "Fern-rock" was another pile, carpeted with beautiful ferns. Then "Lookout-rock" was situated on the verge of the mountain slope, and the missionary children used to climb it to watch the coming of messengers from the city. Distant from the camp was another immense pile of rocks containing a cave, which was called the "Bear-den," suggested by the fact that bears were often seen there. It did not require a vivid imagination to surround some of these formations with stories of ancient ruined castles and battlements, the scenes of once bitter strifes. An, in fact, the mountain abounded in native traditions of ancient peoples who chose it for their stronghold.

Primeval forests covered the mountain, the lofty trees of which were bound together at their tops by creepers, thereby forming a grateful shade. Here, also, was the home of the banyan tree, whose fantastic rootlets, climbing over the boulders, or falling from the lower branches and forming new trunks, afforded much interest. Each tree constituted a grove in itself, and made beautiful playhouses for the children.

Fruit-trees also abounded, some of them proving the place to have been formerly inhabited. Among the kinds most prized was one having fruit hanging from its trunk, like bunches of grapes. They were of yellow and crimson colours, and had a delicious acid flavour. The natives and monkeys had no little rivalry in gathering this fruit. Then there was a giant tree covered in its season with a fruit similar to the strawberry in shape and colour, which was of delicious flavour.

Any attempt to describe K'surdo must needs be unsatisfactory, so varied and unique are its attractions. In addition to what has been mentioned, perhaps the crowning scene remains to be noticed. It is the "Betel-nut Orchard." It was situated in a bowl-like depression of the mountain, intertwined with vines. Here a rich soil had produced a variety of flowering shrubs and trees, the most conspicuous of them being Areca palms, which furnish the prized betel-nut of the country. In the centre of the depression were these beautiful palms, tall and slender, crowned with heavy plumes of dark, glossy green leaves, and golden fruit. They contrasted strongly with the surrounding jungle, and presented a scene of surpassing beauty, of which the beholder could never tire.

In the shade of these trees, cool even at noon-day, one could always find a grateful retreat, which was made still more inviting by a stream of clear water that flowed through the orchard, causing the flowering shrubs that lined its banks to flourish with an Eden luxuriance. There were also other shady nooks scattered here and there, inviting both the weary and the studious to their repose. Indeed, the whole mountaintop was like a well-ordered park, its atmosphere perfumed with flowers, and the whole made vocal by the songs of insects and birds. And only they who have experienced the bird-and-insect life of the tropics can appreciate the peculiar charm of their morning and evening concerts.

K'surdo is also the haunt of various wild animals and reptiles. The fierce heat of the plains in the dry season, with the failure of water, drives the animals to this cooler climate with its water supply. Among the more harmless animals were the black and brown bear, several kinds of deer, the elk, and occasionally the bison. Of the deer there was a small, graceful little fellow called the "barking-deer," so named from the peculiar noise it makes when startled. The dreaded tiger and leopard were also occasionally met, drawn thither in pursuit of deer. Moreover, wild hogs roamed through the forests in search of fruit, while troops of monkeys formed a constant source of amusement to the visitors. They seemed to possess almost human discernment: for their curiosity led them to gather about our camp to watch the children at play, and, finding they were disturbed on week-days, they selected Sundays for their visits. Baboons also were sometimes seen, and they looked strangely human at a distance as they ran over the ground. Thus K'surdo furnished abundant entertainment as well as rest.

It was found practicable to take classes of natives to this resort for instruction, or literary work; so that, while resting, there would be no interruption in our missionary work. At first our encampment consisted of bamboo huts; but later, as this proved so good a missionary sanitarium, more permanent dwellings were erected.

Amid such surroundings adventures were daily occurring which prevented all monotony. And what glorious evenings were those when we gathered in the open square of our encampment under the great banyan tree, which spread over us its gently swaying branches and glossy leaves, and all illuminated by our campfire, while the gentle breeze, which always prevailed in the evening, added to our comfort and enjoyment.

Surprises, however, were liable at any time, and some of them were decidedly ludicrous. For instance, a family of civet cats once discovered our chicken coops, and made several attacks upon them. They came through the tree-tops in the evening, and announced their approach by a series of calls. A plan was made for their destruction. The natives were directed to gather heaps of leaves and fire them when the cats began to call. This was to reveal the intruders in the tree-tops, so that we could despatch them. No little excitement was thus aroused, and when one of the largest cats appeared in the banyan tree, directly over the house of one of the missionaries, a well-aimed rifle-shot brought him down. He was much larger than an ordinary cat, and fell like a stone, passing through the grass roof of the house below. It so happened that the housewife was sitting with her feet on a basket of clothes, hushing her little son to sleep, when the cat came through the roof into the basket, spitting and scratching furiously. The affrighted woman naturally fled to the bed for refuge, but was quickly relieved by the removal of the intruder.

VII - ENCOUNTERS WITH WILD BEASTS AND SERPENTS

During my boyhood in Maine, I became ambitious to shoot a bear, but an opportunity never occurred to do this there. And although frequently seeing them about our encampment on K'surdo, my ambition was slow in being gratified. One day a Karen girl was lost in her rambles. This was discovered when she failed to appear at sunset. Parties were at once sent out in every direction, but no trace of her was discovered. Early in the morning, calling a Karen boy to carry an extra gun, I set out for an extended search around the waist of the mountain. Approaching a deep ravine, down which ran a small brook filled with boulders, and its banks lined with small palms and rattans, I heard a noise like the scratching of a fowl. While reaching back to the boy for my shot-gun, I saw what appeared to my excited vision to be a small elephant rushing out of the ravine up the mountain-side. Though not skilful with a rifle, a snap-shot at the fleeing monster went true and stopped his flight. Turning suddenly, he charged directly toward us. Having a repeating rifle, I fired shot after shot at him, perhaps none taking effect. To my great relief, he stopped in the ravine. His loud and laboured breathing showed that he was badly wounded. Looking back for my Karen boy, I saw him calmly loading the double-barrelled shot-gun with bullets. Gathering up my scattered wits, I drew near the wounded bear to get a good sight of him, well supported by my Karen lad. In fact, his bravery rather shamed me, and I pressed forward to get the first shot. That shot pierced the brute's brain and ended his distress. The bear was a monster. It took six strong men to lift him, and they were unable to carry him to camp. This event greatly excited the camp, especially the natives, who esteemed bear steal as the choicest food.

About noon the next day the lost girl walked into camp as calmly as though being lost were with her a common experience.

There is doubtless a strong attraction for adventure to all lovers of the "wild," especially when mixed with a spice of danger. It may be that this is stronger after than before the event; but to look a fierce beast in the face, which is able to crush you in a moment, without afterward trembling with fear, gives one a comfortable feeling of confidence.

One evening, a little before sundown, I set out on my evening stroll in search of some venison for the camp. Our servant, who was cook and man-of-all-work, thought he would like to follow the "master." After crossing several ridges, we drew near a spot where, a few days before, I had seen deer feeding. I had a double-barrelled shot-gun loaded with a heavy charge of buck-shot. The servant was a little in the rear with my rifle. I was walking quietly, and had passed a deep ravine and was climbing a ridge that made down from the mountaintop. I had nearly reached the summit, when a slight noise on my left made me look up; and there was a sight to stir one's blood. Two very large bears were coming slowly down the ridge, swinging their heads from side to side, as is their custom. They were only several rods distant, and yet they had not heard my approach. In such circumstances one thinks quickly. If I had had my rifle, my anxiety would have been less. The first thought was, how to escape. To turn and run would invite pursuit. The next thought was, to climb a tree; but none was near. So, making a virtue of necessity, I was obliged to face the beasts. Slipping an ounce bullet into my gun over the shot, I prepared for what might come.

Meantime they had drawn nearer, and aiming carefully at the head of the larger bear, thinking the smaller one would flee, I fired. The result was the most awful "mix-up" of bruin and bushes I ever saw. He was evidently very uncomfortable; for his roar was full of pain and rage. Fearing he might get straightened out and turn upon us, I hastened back to the servant for my rifle; and with this in hand the battle was soon ended.

Among the varied incidents which contributed to our entertainment, there were some which did not result so happily. Not far from our camp was a beautiful banyan tree of immense size. It bore abundant fruit, about the size of a cherry, which was much sought after by the birds and beasts of the forest. In strolling through the jungle one day, I observed this tree was shedding its fruit, and that large animals were resorting here daily. This promised a comfortable adventure. Burnishing my new Remington rifle, and taking a good supply of cartridges, I went out to the banyan tree early in the evening to get well settled before the animals came to feed. I selected a large rock within easy shooting distance from the tree; and, arranging my blind, I kept a sharp lookout for the coming game. Soon I was surprised to see three large black animals coming over the ridge toward me. Thinking that I had three bears on my hands, I prepared for battle. The leader was very large. They came rapidly over the hill, evidently looking for food, and the leader, a boar of great size, stopped a half-gunshot from me, presenting a beautiful side shot. Resting my rifle on the rock, and taking careful aim at the vital spot on the shoulder, I fired. But I made a mistake, and lost one of the largest wild boars I ever saw. His tusks appeared to be fully six inches in length. Forgetting that a rifle, heavily loaded, will overshoot within the first hundred yards, and is liable to bound when rested on a rock, I did not make the necessary allowance, and so the bullet only cut the bristles on his back. With a savage cry of alarm he threw up his head, and looked for his enemy. Failing to discover me, he took up a slow and dignified trot, as though scorning such an attack, and passed over the hill out of sight. Of the other two, one sprang aside into a thick clump of bushes, leaving in sight only a small black spot. Somewhat chagrined at my first shot, I stood erect in my shelter, and at arm's-length fired a snap-shot at the black spot in the bushes. The wild boar fell dead a few rods from the place where he was hit. The third one had disappeared. The natives declare that the wild boar is more dangerous to meet than even a tiger. Possibly it was better that I had no closer acquaintance with the first than the cutting of a few bristles from his back.

But our experiences were not always agreeable. Harmless as well as dangerous snakes are abhorrent to most persons. These were our chief discomfort; for they were numerous, and formed no small part of our K'surdo life. In our first encampment our house consisted of a two-roomed bamboo bungalow–a dining- and a sleeping-room. One night as we were finishing our evening meal, the mail from America arrived, and as we were reading the letters in the sleeping-room, we heard an unusual noise among the dishes on the table. Looking up to discover the cause, what was our horror to see an enormous snake reaching down from the rafters to help himself to the butter. In doing this he disturbed a spoon in a cup, which gave us the warning. Seizing a rattan cane, I advanced to the attack. The snake evidently did not like my appearance, for he put his head over the edge of the table to look for a place of escape. This enabled me to strike a fatal blow. He was about fourteen feet long, but was not a poisonous kind.

This incident quite upset our faith in the absence of danger in the house, and, as snakes appeared so often in our house, we changed our encampment to a less dangerous locality. Yet here also, in the course of time, we were disturbed by the appearance of reptiles. We had made a more substantial bungalow, building it well up from the ground. Yet one day the house-mother, stepping into the sleeping-room, where the children were playing on the bed, saw hanging from the rafters a large green snake, which was seemingly fascinated by the singing of the children; for he was swaying back and forth, his glittering eyes fixed upon them. The mother had sufficient presence of mind to quietly call the children outside, when the snake was despatched by the Karen boys.

The cooking for the family was partly done on an oil-stove, which was in a corner of the room. One day the mistress of the house saw what she supposed was a roll of cloth, left by the maid, behind the stove. Stooping to remove it, she saw two bright eyes, and thinking it was a frog, she sought a stick to drive it out, when suddenly the "frog" spread out into a snake six or seven feet long. It proved to be a poisonous kind. A few such warnings kept us alert.

The following accounts will show the character of the more dangerous serpents.

Several narrow escapes from a horrible death from serpents have befallen me in my missionary life, which have deeply impressed me with the providential care of our Heavenly Father. One of these was from a python, and a second from a giant cobra. The python, or as sometimes called, the rock snake, is a variety of the boa family, and is often found in Asia, especially in Burma. The bite of this snake is not poisonous. He captures his prey in his strong coils and crushes it, when he swallows it, beginning with the head. He can easily dispose thus of a small deer or pig. They are sometimes found thirty feed in length and are attractively coloured in rhomboidal figures. I once saw one running down a ravine, which could not have been less than twenty-five feet in length. The python is very fierce, and also quick in movement when darting for prey.

This serpent was captured one morning about a mile from the place where it was photographed. Two Karen lads were travelling with me over a mountain covered with old jungle, or that which had been left undisturbed for centuries. It was during the hot season, and the plains were very dry, so the animals had fled into the mountains for cool shade and water. There were in this forest a variety of large and small deer, wild hogs, bears, and other beasts. The forest through which we were going was very dense, some of the trees being from one hundred and fifty to two hundred feet in height. Rattans, small palms, bamboos, and many long-leafed tropical plants grew in rank profusion. The air was heavy with the fragrance of flowering trees and creeping plants, mingled with the rank odour of living creatures. We were expecting at every turn of the brook, along which we were cautiously proceeding, to see some wild animal. We were not looking for serpents, though knowing we were passing through their haunts. I was stepping from rock to rock in the brook, so as to avoid noise which would frighten away game, and my two Karen boys were following at some distance along the bank of the brook. As I put my foot upon a large rock, I noticed a sudden movement among the dry leaves between that rock and a larger one about three feet from it; and at the same time I caught sight of the brilliant colours of this great serpent through the leaves. Quick as thought I sprang to the bank of the brook, but only a few seconds before the enormous folds of this serpent swept over the place on which I had stood. In fact, we had sprang nearly together; though I was, most fortunately, slightly ahead of the snake. Immediately I put a fatal shot through his neck.

The wisdom of the serpent was here clearly shown; for he had coiled himself closely between the rocks, and covered himself with dry leaves, so that he could easily capture any animal passing up or down the brook. For such an animal would naturally step over either of the rocks, and so into the coils of the monster. And he surely would have caught me, if I had not seen him as quickly as I did. My two Karen boys were greatly excited, and most joyous over the escape of their teacher. Their joy was also heightened by the thought of the coming feast; for they declared the flesh of the python was like that of the chicken. They coiled him on a long bamboo, and it required their united strength, with frequent rests, to carry him to camp.

There is only one serpent in all India, so far as I know, which will pursue human beings for the purpose of attack. The family of adders, which are very poisonous, strike only when disturbed, and then in self-defence. So with the cobra, of the hooded family of snakes. The family of the cobra de capello, the individuals of which sometimes attain a length of six feet, is very numerous, but very seldom attack a person. Usually, when suddenly disturbed, they lift their head, spread the hood, which is an enlargement of the skin of the neck, and utter a sharp hissing sound, which serves as a warning; though a strike often follows closely after the hiss.

Once I nearly stepped on one of these snakes, but, warned by the hiss, I saw the reptile at my feet with uplifted head and spread hood, ready to strike me. A quick side jump saved me from the bite. I should not have seen him, as I was walking in thick brush, but for the warning hiss.

There is, however, no snake in the hooded family so dangerous, and greatly to be dreaded, as the giant cobra, or hamadryad. This serpent sometimes attains the length of thirteen feet. It is very quick in its motions, can swim, and also climb trees. The natives declare it can glide along on level ground as fast as a horse can run. As it cannot hold on to sloping ground, the natives, when pursued by this serpent, take to the hill-sides for escape. Fortunately, the giant cobra is not very common in India, and his marking is so like a "jail-bird" that he is readily distinguished from his surroundings. This marking, in the case I am about to relate, consisted of dark-brown and dirty-grey bands of about one and a half inches in width, alternating from head to tail.

One morning I was travelling alone through the forest, hunting wild chickens. Flocks of jungle fowl, like the Brahma fowl seen in this country, as well as pheasants of gay plumage, were often met, scratching among the leaves under clumps of bamboos for bamboo seed. Every morning the cocks would be heard challenging each other with their vigorous crowing. I had previously seen a flock of these fowls in that locality. It was near the close of the dry season, when the dry leaves of the trees had fallen on the ground, and any movement among them could be easily heard for some distance. As I strolled along, listening for any jungle noise, I heard a rustling of the leaves, as if a hen were scratching for her breakfast; and I stopped at once to locate its direction. When I stopped the noise ceased, and I moved a gain. Again I heard the rustling sound, and turned to locate it. The third time I was somewhat startled: for it seemed that whatever was making the noise was timing its motions with my own. This caused me to look back along the way over which I had come, and there, indeed, was the source of the sound that had startled me. It was a giant cobra, the hamadryad, of which I had been told so many frightful stories by the natives, and he was after me. I had no time to study the serpent, for he was only a few feet distant, and had evidently been stalking me, to get near enough for attack before being seen. When he saw that he was observed, he raised his great head about three feet from the ground and spread his great hood, his challenge for a battle. A quick shot hit him as he sprang at me, and his swift contortions were for the moment frightful to behold. A second shot reached a vital spot, and he dropped dead at my feet. Then, as I realised how near I had come to a sudden and frightful death, a cold chill swept over me. Again the providential care of the Heavenly Father had delivered me from an awful death, and a feeling of deep gratitude filled my heart. Had I not been prompt to look backward over my path, I should have lost my life. The serpent was ten and a half feet long.

VIII - STORY OF THE YAHDO CHAPEL

Northeast from Toungoo, in Burma, four hard days' journey through jungle and over mountain trails, lies the large Karen village of Yahdo; which has become historic in the Toungoo Mission. When our missionary work was first planned, this part of the country was quite unknown. It was located on the boundary line between English and independent territory. Here the dividing mountain range towered six thousand feet above the sea. At the point where Yahdo was situated these mountains branched southward, as the fore-finger and thumb of the left hand, and the Yahdo valley nestled between them.

This lovely valley was about three miles long and one mile wide. A laughing mountain stream runs through the centre of the valley, its banks fringed with willows and flowers of the temperate zone. In passing from the lower ranges into this valley, the change from tropical into temperate-zone scenery was so sudden as to be startling. The bounding mountain ranges also greatly differed from the surrounding ones. Those answering to the thumb had rounded tops and graceful slopes, while those answering to the forefinger were ragged, precipitous, and broken. Their sharp, towering peaks, and their precipitous crags, from eight hundred to a thousand feet in height, formed a scene of imposing grandeur.

When the plans for our missionary work were prepared, we aimed to reach the frontier in our evangelistic tours as soon as possible; yet it took many years to explore and occupy the intervening territory. At that time, 1866, the frontier church was named Shwaynangyee, which was gathered by Dr. M. H. Bixby, afterwards pastor of Cranston Street Baptist Church, Providence, R. I. It was situated in a tribe which proved to be of the Karen race, called Gaicho Karens, though at the time it was gathered, it was thought to belong to another race.

The first work of the new missionary, who succeeded Dr. Bixby, was to visit this church. It was found to be admirably located for our advance to the northeast. We strengthened the school and the hands of the pastor, who proved to be a wise pioneer and faithful preacher of the gospel. In a few years there was a call for an advance from this point. Several villages had been won for Christ by this teacher at Shwaynangyee, and among them was one a long day's journey to the northeast, named Prehso. This in turn was made a frontier station, or centre from which teachers and evangelists were sent forth, and it grew to be one of the strongest churches in the Toungoo district. It was situated at the foot of the great dividing range on which Yahdo was located.

While subsequently visiting this church on a tour of inspection, a delegation came over the mountains to ask us for teachers to go to the Yahdo valley.

That was a glad morning for us, for though we had never visited that valley, we had often cast our eyes on those towering mountains, and longed to plant the flag of the gospel on their heights. As these two valleys were more or less at enmity with each mother, the trail over the mountains had fallen into disuse, and the natives thought it doubtful if I could get my pony over the hills. But with a good company of followers, provided with long knives, we set out on the climb. The trail was of the worst kind. Fallen trees had to be cut and moved; railings were placed along the precipitous sides of the mountain to guard the ponies from falling; and sometimes we could ascend only by clinging with both hands and feet. After several hours of such effort, we came out upon the ridge of the thumb, and there unrolled before us one of the most beautiful scenes in all the Toungoo hills. A brook, flowing merrily southward, invited us to follow its course. The three villages, two to the north and one to the south, without a single Christian disciple, were entreating us to come to their help.

As we stood on that ridge, studying the landscape before us, we were deeply impressed by the importance of this valley as a strategic point from which to advance the cause of Christ in these hills; and, feeling that God's set time had come to begin this work, we registered in our hearts a firm resolve to undertake it; though with slight conception of the strong opposition the great enemy of Christ would rally against us. How little did we realise that the coming of Christ's messenger would rouse the demon of war in this seeming abode of peace. But such was our destined experience. Already the opposing forces were beginning to gather. And here we may remark that, in all our missionary life, every endeavour to win a territory for Christ from the kingdom of darkness has encountered the most strenuous and persistent opposition.

Passing over the ridge of the thumb, we descended into the valley. How beautiful it was! And yet how marred by the life of heathenism. All men went about with matchlocks, spears, and swords. We found the middle of the valley covered with a dense swamp. Around the edges were beautiful fields of rice, and the mountain stream lost none of its attractions on nearer approach. Crossing the valley, we ascended the hill on which was located the largest village, Yahdo, or Wahthaucho, the former meaning "the big plantain-hill," and the latter "the crown of large bamboos." Both names were equally applicable. The beautiful, large bamboo, which grows in masses and to the height of one hundred or more feet, crowned the whole hilltop with its wavy plumes. As we advanced through the avenue formed by these graceful trees, the sight was entrancing. Though our reception was cordial, we soon found that the old blood feuds were liable to break out at any time. Roman Catholic priests were already using these to influence the minds of the people against each other. The nominal worship of Christ was only a counter-movement to the evil actions of the priests.

In crossing the valley and ascending the hill to the village, we were surrounded by a great concourse of wild men and women. The village was encompassed by a stockade and ditch. Owing to the multitude of dogs and pigs, and the curious people pressing about us, our camp was pitched just outside the stockade. And, as tigers and other wild beasts infested the country, it was thought unsafe to remain in camp alone, so a company of young men came at dusk, built fires, and spread their mats on the ground all around our camp. The week spent at this place was full of work. The people cheerfully followed our lead. The three villages of the valley were called together, and a covenant entered into for future mutual work and help. A school was organised at once with children from two of the villages. A more happy beginning of a new interest in the line of Christian civilisation we never witnessed.

It seemed for once that the enemy of all righteousness had failed to take notice of this entrance into his kingdom. But, no. A company of Roman Catholic priests quickly followed us to the Yahdo valley, and, with the skill of which they are masters, they scattered seeds of doubt, and alienated two of the villages from their peace compact. While we clung to the village of Yahdo, and kept up a flourishing school, the other two villages were led into open hostility. Old blood feuds, long since buried, were reopened and spurred into activity. These feuds involved not only the villages in Yahdo valley, but some eight or more others across the English frontier. The priests had formed an alliance with one of the most notorious robbers and freebooters in all the mountains, named Murr. In him they found a zealous instrument for carrying out their purpose, which was evidently our expulsion from the Yahdo valley.

One morning nine persons from a neighbouring village, friendly to Yahdo, were seized while passing the village to the City of Toungoo for trade, and were carried off to a stronghold, where they were held for ransom. Live stock belonging to Yahdo was frequently killed, or mutilated, and all means known to the heathen for annoying the little band of Yahdo disciples and their associates were used. The division among the Karens had now assumed large proportions. The enemy grew bold and defiant, because of the non-resistant attitude of the Yahdo people, and the mistaken supposition that the valley was outside of English territory, and that they were thus free to do whatever they liked.

In September, 1883, the trouble culminated in a pitched battle between the friends of the Yahdo people and the party championed by the priests, in which seven of that party were killed and their village burned to the ground.

This was loudly charged to the pastor of the Yahdo church by the priests, and the whole question was now brought to the attention of the English government. We were forced by circumstances to ask for an official investigation. As the result, the judge, an English officer, pronounced the Yahdo Christians and their pastor to be entirely innocent of wrong-doing, and also deserving of great praise for the forbearance and moderation they had exhibited. Hereupon the priests charged the judge with being prejudiced by our people, and by false evidence on our part; but he declared in unmistakable terms, "I form my decision on testimony of your own people, which you have given me." On further evidence, the chief of the party opposed to us was arrested, tried for murder and dacoity, convicted, and sent into exile. A police guard was also placed in Yahdo for the further protection of the people. This was necessary from the fact that the official investigation showed that Yahdo was not outside the British boundary, as we had supposed; for it lay between the thumb and the forefinger of the mountain range, as already mentioned. This was a crushing blow to the power of the priests in that quarter.

As no open violation of the law would now be safe, our enemies resorted to petty annoyances. But, notwithstanding such persecutions, the village grew to be very prosperous. The little chapel, which the people had laboriously built, and the school of sixty pupils therein gathered, were a crown of glory to the village. They loved their chapel with a love grown large from the sacrifices they had made in building it. But the time of sorest trial was at their door.

One bright but windy morning, the opposing village, now located on the thumb of the mountain system, set their fields of felled trees on fire, evidently with the intention of destroying Yahdo village on the opposite side of the valley, and thus escaping all blame, charging it to the wind. The southwest monsoon was strongly blowing; and as the flames mounted into the air, brands were caught up by the wind, carried across the valley, and rained upon the roofs of the houses in Yahdo. In less than half an hour, more than eighty houses, with their shade-trees, stores of food, everything, were reduced to ashes. The beautiful chapel, of which they were so justly proud, was also utterly destroyed.

Said the teacher in a written statement: "Our chapel, which cost us so much labour and money, our crown of delight, our glory, in which we rejoiced, was utterly destroyed in a few minutes, together with the books and school apparatus. The weeping women and the children were heart-broken as they beheld this destruction of their chapel; and as I saw their great sorrow, my throat filled, and I could not breathe, and had to turn away from the sad sight for relief.... Therefore," the letter concludes, "dear brothers in Christ, remember us, your youngest church, in your prayers to Christ, in our affliction." Signed, "Your brother in Christ, Tah Dee."

Sau Lee, Brec Missionary

Tah Dee, Yahdo Pastor

We hastened from Toungoo to the scene of the fire as soon as possible. And as we stood looking over the charred hill-top, with its glory of bamboo and tamarind trees in ashes, and saw our beloved disciples about their brush huts, striving to get together something with which to begin life anew, for the moment the shadow of the wing of the great tempter fell across my vision. For fifteen years we had wrought incessantly to capture this stronghold in the mountains for the Kingdom of our Lord. Already the benign influence of this little church was felt among the heathen in the north and northwest, even to distant Karenni. We had dreamed of the time when the blood feuds of these many tribes would be annihilated; when peace would reign over these mountains; when witchcraft would be destroyed, and the songs of praise to God, would take the place of all this discord. And here, in one short half-hour, these hopes were reduced to ashes.

But the evil shadow of the wing quickly passed, as the promises of God began to shine forth. The memory of Divine help in the past reassured us; and, as the beloved disciples rallied around us, we found ourselves cheerfully discussing ways and means for building a new chapel. We planned a larger and more beautiful building than the former. It was to be thirty-six by twenty-four feet, two stories, and having a tower, in which we already by faith heard a bell calling the people to worship. In a few days the plans took complete form. Nine hundred sticks of timber must be cut and brought from the forest, about two miles distant. Eight thousand shingles must be brought from Toungoo, besides nails, glass, etc. Men must also be hired to saw the lumber. Then came the question of individual work. The disciples were inclined to ask the heathen to help them. But when we suggested that this ought to be a love offering unto the Lord on the part of the disciples, and when they read what God said to Zerubbabel in rebuilding the temple, that "it was not by might, nor by power, but by My Spirit, saith the Lord," they decided to do all the work themselves.

There were in all about forty disciples. They had lost nearly everything; but, after much consultation, they pledged one hundred and eighty-five rupees towards the work, and in addition to this the men promised each thirty days' labour, and the women fifteen days, in building the house of God. They declared, "We wish to do this for Christ's sake." It was no easy work to do all the work involved with their own hands; and yet they undertook it with cheerfulness.

In the meantime there was rejoicing of another kind across the valley. When the enemy saw the destruction of the village chapel, they were filled with fiendish joy and exultation. They railingly asked the stricken disciples: "Where now is your God? He has burned your village and has left you nothing. He has scattered your people. Where is your glory?" "But," said the disciples among themselves, "we will build a new chapel, better than the last, to the glory of our God." So they bowed their heads humbly to the reviling of their enemies, and went on with their work. For a whole year they endured this reviling. But God was pleased with their faith, and was preparing a great and glorious deliverance.

Almost a year after the chapel was burned, a missionary wrote to a friend in Philadelphia, mentioning in his letter the situation of this bereaved church. The way still looked difficult, but with our little band of zealous disciples we were struggling on by faith in God. This letter reached its destination–the wife of a prominent pastor in Philadelphia. She read it to a little mission band at the Second Germantown Baptist Church, and her letter will best tell the story. I am sure she will pardon its insertion here: "The children were deeply interested, and wanted to do what they could to help. That evening, in our home at the parsonage, little Rob, dear boy, came to me saying: 'Mother, here is something for you to help rebuild the chapel at Yahdo, where Dr. Bunker is'; and, handing me a bright twenty-five-cent piece, he ran out of the room. I called him back, and said, knowing what little money he had was already spent, 'Why, Robbie, dear, where did you get this money?' 'Sold my little Bunny, mother;' and he tried to look very brave, for that rabbit was a great pet of his; it had not been sold without a great deal of self-denial."

At a subsequent meeting of the Children's Missionary Band, one hundred and seventy-five dollars were contributed. Then Dr. Wayland opened his paper, The National Baptist, for a public appeal, which raised the sum to five hundred dollars. Thus the marvellous goodness of God answered the faith of these few disciples in Yahdo more bountifully than we could ask or even think.

The chapel was finished, and in due time Dr. Bixby, of Cranston Street Baptist Church, Providence, R. I., sent his bell for the tower. So this new temple of worship, much more beautiful than the other one destroyed by fire, was completed amidst great rejoicing, and was christened the "Mary Love" Chapel of Yahdo.

IX - THIRTEEN WITCHES

Among the superstitions which curse the hill tribes of Burma, one of the most cruel is witchcraft. No superstition of old New England could surpass this work of the evil one in the hills of Burma. And the strangest thing is that the crime is usually charged to old women. Among tribes where there is no law, save that of the strongest, the victims of this superstition have no redress. Wherever sickness has broken out, or a series of misfortunes has befallen the people, it requires little effort to start a cry of witchcraft as their cause. The slightest occasion for directing the suspicion of those who suffer towards some old woman who has passed her usefulness, or who has aroused enmity among her neighbours by her sharp tongue, is enough to seal her fate.

The beginning of such strife results in charge and countercharge, until not only families, but sometimes whole villages are broken up. If the party that brings the charge against some old mother is the stronger, it often results in the banishment of the victim from the village, or in her condemnation and death, the whole family sometimes becoming involved. At such times the condemned are driven outside the village and speared or shot to death, and their bones are left to bleach in the sun. Such gruesome sights have often been seen by missionaries in their tours among these hills.

On the borders between English territory and the Independent States eastward from Toungoo, there is one of the most fruitful churches of the Bghai Karen Mission. It is located in a valley near the top of the Poungloung mountain ranges, on one of the main roads to the interior, and amid the most picturesque scenery. The fame of this church had spread into all the surrounding region. The savage people were telling each other how this village of Yahdo had given up its old customs, and had chosen the new life, the life of Yuah (God). The reports were that they had become women instead of men, who would no longer fight; that they were kind to all strangers who came into their village, and especially that they received and protected all refugees from other villages, who had been charged with witchcraft and had been expelled from their homes. So widespread had this last report become that many old women under this charge of witchcraft sought refuge in Yahdo. They were given employment in such domestic work as they were able to perform in exchange for their food.

One hot season the missionaries went to Yahdo as a place of rest, where they found thirteen of these poor women. Together they formed one of the most pitiful sights seen among these hills. The condition of women among the Toungoo heathen is one of great hardship and suffering at best; for they are compelled not only to raise their large families of children, and care for their households, but are also obliged to help cultivate the fields. It is common among the heathen Karens to see the mother of the family digging out weeds with a short-handled hoe, and at the same time carrying a baby on her back, wrapped in a cotton blanket, while another child drags at her skirts. At the age of twenty-five or thirty years she looks to be sixty or seventy. Yet as long as she has the love of her children and the savage love, it may be, of her husband, her life is not wholly void of comfort. When, however, worn out with her hard life, her hold on her husband's affections weakens, and her children have grown up and left the home, her lot often sinks into utter wretchedness. If now, through an enemy's malice, or her husband's desire for a new wife, the cry of "witch" is raised against her, the bitterest possible cup is pressed to her lips. She is compelled to flee from her home and people, or perish by violence. Perhaps as you see her dull and stupid look, you feel that the finer feelings of the mother do not vibrate with pain at such a separation; but even a dog will leave home with reluctance. Bent over by years of double labour, with a spear in her hand for a staff, as well as for protection, she takes her weary way toward that Christian village, of which she has heard the people talk, where they do not kill old women under the charge of witchcraft. After days of toilsome journeying, spending her nights either in the jungle or some village, she reaches Yahdo, and we see her among the thirteen witches.

The two women missionaries of our party were strongly moved in their sympathies for this company of outcasts. They commenced with peculiar tact to cultivate their acquaintance, and in a short time won their confidence. They took occasion to meet them when they were at their work, feeding the pigs, or pounding out the family rice from its husks, or preparing food for cooking. It was little they could do, bowed and broken down by past sufferings, but they could appreciate the kindness these women were showing them.

Finally they were gathered into the Sunday school and formed the "infant class." This title caused some merriment among the Sunday-school children. They occupied one corner of the chapel, sitting close together on the floor. It was a picture, once seen, never to be forgotten. Their delight at being numbered among the Sunday-school children was almost pitiful. The missionary teacher wrote for them on a blackboard in large letters, as some were nearly blind, a sentence of three words in Karen, "Yuah me taheh" ("God is love"). They were urged to trace out the letters and observe their form; and, by patient instruction, they were in time able to distinguish them from anything else when put upon the board. As it flashed upon them that they were able to read this sentence like other scholars in the school, their delight was almost boundless. But the truth contained in these words was more difficult to apprehend. They had some basis in their traditions, on which to form their knowledge of Yuah, but His character as an ever-present and all-wise Father was new to them. This word mastered, however, they found it more difficult to understand that He was "love." All their experience seemed to deny the thought. "Why," said some of them, "how can Yuah, who made the bright sun, as you say, love men?" But when they came to see the next lesson, "Yuah eh yah," which means, "God loves me," the struggle between a budding faith and their life-long experience was wonderful to behold. "Why," said some of them, "this says God loves me. I am only an old, worn-out woman. I can no longer dig in the fields, nor cook food for my family. My husband no longer loves me; for he joined others in driving me from my village as a witch. If I had remained in the village, he would have joined others in taking my life." "Yes," said another, "my children no longer love me. How I wrought for them night and day, hoping they would care for me in my old age; but they have helped to drive me from my home." "Oh," said another, "there is no love!"

Their past sufferings were engraven on their faces. These had hardened them beyond tears, and now obscured the bright light of that little sentence which these messengers of God were trying to teach them–"God loves me."

During the several weeks the missionaries were among them, these so-called "witches" made real progress in the new life. Little by little they apprehended the great love of God, even for them, and some of the number manifestly came to apprehend the fact of their little Sunday-school lesson–"God loves me."

No clearer proof of the Divine agency in the enlightenment of these old women could be desired than the marvellous change which took place in them as they came to realise God's love for them. They repeated the lesson over and over to themselves and to each other; they regarded it as one would good news, long desired, from a far country. A perceptible change took place in their whole bearing; a new light came into their dim eyes; and a cheerfulness, unknown before, enlivened them. The unanimous verdict of the missionaries who saw them was, "This is the work of God."

At the close of the season, on the departure of the missionary women to their work in town, an examination of the Sunday school at Yahdo was held. It was a large and enthusiastic school, but no class displayed more enthusiasm than the "infant class." The examination revealed that most of them had completely mastered their two lessons, and what grew out of them. No child in the school showed more pride than they in their examination.

Some one conceived the idea of giving rewards of merit to the "infant class." As there was nothing better at hand, little squares were cut out of a biscuit tin and covered with white paper. Two holes were punched in each, through which were run bright coloured threads, by which to suspend them. On these tickets were written the two sentences, which were of such moment to them. No class of Sunday-school children in any Christian land were ever more pleased with their beautiful cards and costly books than were these thirteen deserted grandmothers. When these tickets were placed in their hands, no words can express the joy and praise that animated the school at the sight. In conclusion, nine of the number soon applied for admission to the church at Yahdo, and were baptised. And most of them became active workers. And yet how hopeless was their case, if left to mere human aid. Surely, their experience presents a bright comment on the declaration made by Isaiah concerning the Christ and which He himself adopted: "The Spirit of the Lord God is upon me; because the Lord hath anointed me to preach good tidings unto the meek: He hath sent me to bind up the broken-hearted, to proclaim liberty to the captives, and the opening of the prison to them that are bound."

X - PERILS AND PLEASURES

Early mission travel in Burma, either by water or by land, was far more difficult than in these days of railways and government roads. Especially was this true in the pioneer stations. At these stations missionary journeys were undertaken on foot, or with a pony or elephant. The luggage for the trip was carried by native bearers in baskets on their backs. The roads for the most part were narrow, winding foot-paths, through the dense jungle of the plains, and up the sides of steep mountains, sometimes along the beds of brooks or on the ridges of the mountains, subject to all the roughness of the country. If, occasionally, a part of the journey could be made by boat, this was counted great gain. Our supplies were of the most economical character, for the reason that it was costly and inconvenient to employ a large number of bearers. Hence the outfit for a missionary journey was usually reduced to the smallest amount necessary for health and effective work. Among native Christians, supplies of rice, some vegetables, eggs, and poultry could always be found. But as the natives of Burma are quite as fond of "ripe" eggs as fresh, these had always to be tested before cooking. Thus equipped with cooking utensils and provisions, clothes, books, and medicines, more or less according to the length of the journey, we undertook our missionary tours. Camp was made wherever night overtook us. A small tent was sufficient to shield from falling dew and night air.

As wood abounded, the natives built large fires, both for comfort and protection. Wild beasts are sometimes numerous and aggressive. When travelling through old jungle, venomous insects and serpents are troublesome. Often times the missionary journey can be so arranged as to pass each night in some Christian or heathen village. But many pleasant nights will often be spent in the grand, primeval forest, where one is lulled to sleep by the soft music of the graceful bamboo, or the heavier music of the wind blowing through the tops of the giant trees. In the early morning, after such a night, one is often wakened by the chattering of monkeys in the tree-tops, the screaming flocks of paraquets seeking their feeding-grounds, or the call of the cook to breakfast, and the new day begins.

In this method of mission travel, however, one could not always forecast the difficulties he must encounter, and so provide for them. Unlooked-for hardships were often experienced.

In the early days the Association of the Karen churches of the Toungoo country, on one occasion, was held in the extreme northern part of the mission field, several days' journey from the city. A party of several missionaries, with native assistants, was planned for the purpose of attending this Association. The first two days could be made by boat, the balance of the journey being through primitive forest and jungle. Owing to exigencies of mission work at the time, it was necessary for me to delay my departure for one day, and on the next, follow the party on land. This necessitated taking two days' journey in one. My luggage went with the main party by boat, the understanding being that we should overtake them at the end of the second day's journey. The plan looked simple enough, but the sequel justified the axiom, "In jungle travel never separate from your supplies even for an hour."

It was nearly ten o'clock on the second day after the departure of the party before I was able to continue my journey. Our little party consisted of three Karens and two native ponies. The road was fairly good all the way along the bank of the Sittang River. At noontime we hoped to secure food at some native village, but could find only rice and a little salt fish. During the afternoon we travelled rapidly, but failed to reach the appointed stopping-place before ten o'clock. Our ponies were worn out and unable to bear us. One who has been weary to the point of sinking can easily imagine how eagerly we looked for our boat and supplies. As we came into the village, we saw the boat moored at the bank, but how great was our surprise to find it abandoned and empty. Through some misunderstanding the party had taken their departure towards the mountains without leaving any trace, save the broad path which led into the great forest.

Owing to the danger of fever, and because we had no supplies, we took the only course open to us–this path which led in the direction of the village where the meetings were to be held. About three o'clock in the morning, after an all-night's journey, we judged from the signs about us that we were drawing near to a village; but the branch roads were so confusing we signalled, in hope of reaching the ears of our friends. Three guns were discharged in quick succession, and we listened for an answering sound. The distant sound of a gong showed that our signal had been heard, and we hastened on with renewed hope in the direction of the sound. As we entered a thicker part of the forest, where the moonlight was shut out by the overhanging tree-tops, we met with our greatest surprise of the night. We were journeying along the territory between the English possessions and those of the Independent States. As we were about to enter a deep ravine, which lay across our path, a file of native police suddenly arose, not more than six rods distant, and fired a volley at us point-bank. I was in the lead when this firing took place. If they had not been such poor shots, we should all have suffered. Our Karen associates were terribly frightened, and shouted, "Come back, teacher, run, we are all dead men!" The teacher did run–but the other way. He dashed in among the police, before they could reload, and the waving of an English "topee," or sun hat, and a few vigorous words in their own tongue, quickly brought them to their knees. For, being policemen, they had violated one of the government rules, which required them to challenge before firing. With the guidance of this now very willing band, we soon reached the village where the police force was stationed.

The weariness of the party can be better imagined than described. Here we were again disappointed, not finding our friends; but our informants told us that there were a party of white people at a village nearby. We were able to find a few eggs for our refreshment, and an armful of straw to sleep on. A messenger was sent off to find who these white men were, and to inform our party, if it were they, of our arrival. In about an hour messengers returned with a bottle of tea, and we all went to join the main party. A whole day's sleep and a few doses of anti-fever medicine enabled us to join the march for the place of our destination. Our resolution, "to never be separated from our supplies even for an hour," was greatly strengthened by this experience.

Red Karen Grandmother

Red Karen Woman

But travel in pioneer work in mission life was by no means all hardship. Our close touch with nature was a constant delight. Rare scenes of mountain and plain frequently added to our enjoyment as we passed slowly through the great forest or along the mountain ridges. There was a wonderful variety of flowering trees, and on the mountaintops many large trees were festooned with beautiful and fragrant orchids, which our native followers gathered for us in great quantities. Often their fragrance filled the air with rich perfume. Strange grasses and ferns delighted us in every ravine; as well as dwarf palms, begonias, and other flowering plants.

Naturally, some scenes would specially imprint themselves upon our memory, of which the following is an example: We were crossing the Shan hills in the month of December, when the dry season was well established. Our course lay over the highest range of mountains between the Toungoo and Salwen rivers. They were covered with beautiful pines and a semi-tropical growth. Wild apple-trees, loaded with blossoms, filled the air with a perfume familiar to our home-land. Our journey began early in the morning. The air was clear and invigorating. As we reached the top of the range, travelling eastward, we were greeted by the rising sun, and our hearts were filled with joy and praise as we watched it flooding the thousand hills with its golden rays. Passing beneath a dense pine grove, and turning a headland on the eastern slope of the hills, we beheld a scene of surpassing loveliness, which caused our whole party to halt. Pen cannot describe the rare beauty unfolded before us.

Far below was a great amphitheatre surrounded by hills. A dark shadow enfolded its depths, and around and above this was spread a thick mantle of sparkling hoarfrost. The surrounding mountains were bathed in bright sunshine, and on the eastern side fell away, thus letting the light shine in upon the amphitheatre. The mountains were covered with groups of low pines, which made rich contrasts of colour with the grey of the rocks and dried grasses, the jet black of a portion which had been burned by recent fires, the sparkling frost in the amphitheatre, and the light green of a large grove of giant bamboos in the background, in which there nestled a native village with its straw-coloured roofs. Then this vivid picture was intensified by a group of yellow-robed priests, who came into view on the right, and passed along the middle ground toward a cluster of white pagodas on the left. A large grove of blossoming cherry trees in the immediate foreground added their delicate beauty to the scene. The golden rays of the rising sun blended the whole picture into one harmonious whole.

This scene remained with us for many years, and often gave us cheer, when good-cheer was needed. Scenes like this are among the rich rewards with which the pioneer missionary and lover of nature is often blessed.

XI - THE MIRACLE OF SENITE

There have been, and of necessity always will be, two distinct features of missionary work, as viewed from a material or spiritual standpoint. The root principle of all such work is of Divine origin. It has its birth and rise in the heart and work of Jesus Christ, the Son of God. Being Divine, it cannot be subjected to human rules and reasoning. Nor can it be understood in its working by those who do not thus receive it. Hence we claim that all reasoning about the "Naturalisation of Religion" to certain races, or its adaptation to the thought and customs of different nations, is contrary to the very genius of Christianity, because they are all "of the earth earthy." We have said that the root principle of the religion of Jesus is Divine, and it is natural that the results of such working should also be of a Divine character, and therefore miraculous. When the Lord declared to Nicodemus, "Ye must be born again," neither he nor his followers during all the centuries have been able to understand this declaration. Yet the missionary, having first experienced this miraculous work of the Holy Spirit, has been permitted to gaze with delight upon its repetition in the experiences of converted heathen. The young missionary, however, who has witnessed this miracle in individual cases in his own land, in his first missionary experience, may wonder if, in the dark-minded and ignorant savage before him, he can ever hope to see a like miracle. Supporters of missions also have an abiding interest in all exhibitions of the Holy Spirit's power as related in the reports from mission fields. The following account of the regeneration of a village of savages in the Toungoo hills of Burma has more than ordinary interest in this connection.

The mountainous country between the Toungoo and Salwen rivers is inhabited by a number of Karen tribes who are very wild and are a law unto themselves. They are in almost constant feudal warfare, the stronger preying upon the weaker. Or this was their condition when the events here narrated took place.

Six days eastward from Toungoo City, in the heart of this country, a large village named Senite had its stronghold. It was a veritable fortress, consisting of a gigantic limestone cliff rising more than three hundred feet above the surrounding country. Three sides of this cliff were almost perpendicular, and could be ascended only by a very rough, steep, and difficult path, which required the use of both hands and feet. The people on the cliff numbered about four hundred, dwelling in rude bamboo huts. They had taken refuge on the top of this rock because they had made enemies in the surrounding country by their life of violence and crime. Living in such a locality, wood and water were difficult to obtain, and this work fell to the lot of the women and children.

When part way up the hill, the mission party became weary with the hard climbing, and stopped in the mouth of a cave to rest. While there, some of the village women came up the hill, bearing heavy loads of wood and water. As they had never seen a white man before, they were overcome with astonishment, and we were equally surprised at the strange appearance of the women. Their ornaments of brass wire, worn about their necks and limbs, made them most extraordinary looking creatures. The wire was about half an inch in diameter and was put on in regular coils, increasing in number as the women grew older. This caused the neck to lengthen to an unusual degree, and the pressing wire made the jaw-bone project, giving a most repulsive effect, though regarded by them as a mark of great beauty. Their gait also, because of the heavy coils around their legs, was very awkward. Besides the wire, they were weighted by several pounds of different coloured beads, and a variety of charms, metallic and otherwise, were hung around their necks. Their hair was done up on top of their heads in a pyramid form, and held in place by silver pins and combs. How they could carry such heavy loads up that steep hillside, thus hampered, was a marvel to us; and the marvel was increased when we found it was difficult to lift one of their loads from the ground.

When they first saw us, fear sent them rushing back, but a few kind words in their own tongue, from a native pastor, reassured them, and they soon passed on up the cliff to the village. We followed, using our hands to help us up the rough way, and came shortly to the level top of the cliff, where we were met by the villagers. The excitement among them was very great, for this was the first time a white man had visited them. Soon two tents were pitched, and the little organ opened. Our Karen school-boys and girls now sang their beautiful hymns, to the delight of the listeners.

At first, the many pigs and dogs, and the excitement of the people caused great confusion. Soon, however, the music had a quieting effect, and those who sat on the platform with the singers were able to look about them and study the scene. We saw before us the result of years of savagery, ignorance, and superstition. On every hand were signs of fetish worship. Skulls of various animals were hung on bamboos in every available place, to ward off evil spirits, which the people feared might cause accident or sickness among them. Small baskets of bamboo filled with eggs (very old), and other articles of food, were placed at all the entrances of the village for a like purpose. Bamboo altars were also placed about the village with rice beer for the entertainment of spirits, which were supposed to be hovering about.

While the children were singing, all the villagers came together, forming a semicircle around the little company of Christians. Fear had given place to the keenest curiosity on their faces. The small children formed the lower circle, those of larger growth above them, while the men and women were above all, forming a wall of black eyes and savage faces, presenting a sight never to be forgotten. It would not be strange if some messenger of the gospel, looking upon such a scene of hopelessness and stupidity, should question the ability of the gospel to lift such human beings into the beauty and glory of the Christ-life. Certainly no ground could be more utterly laid waste by the evil one for the experiment. This experiment was now to be made, and the work had already begun.

After the confusion had been somewhat quieted by the music, a young native preacher, familiar with their language, stepped forward, and announced the good news from Jesus our Lord, which we had come to give them. He told them of the greatness and goodness of Jehovah, whom they knew in their tradition as "Yuah," and of the forgiveness of sin, concerning which they had never heard, and thought to be impossible; how the Son of God had come from heaven to earth, and had borne their sins away, because of His great love for them.

The people were at once interested. No story can so quickly lay hold of the savage mind and rivet attention as this story of the glad tidings. And this fact was here emphasised. For the young man had experienced the truth of the story, and he spoke with such emotion as to commend his message to his hearers.

It was most interesting to watch the play of emotion upon their stolid faces, stepped as the people were in sin, ignorance, and violence. For the first time they were hearing a voice from heaven. No other voice could possibly awaken in their souls such a Divine response. It was another miracle of grace, which we watched through subsequent years with the keenest interest. Could the love of Jesus of Nazareth, as displayed upon the cross, reach the hearts of such as these, and change them into Christian children?

It was evident that the young preacher had made a favourable impression upon his audience; for when he finished, a lively discussion broke out among the people. Some said: "We want this God for our God. If He loves men, let Him come and live among us." Others objected: "If He dwells among us, we can make no more raids for plunder among other villages, and our enemies will come and devour us." Others said, "Yes, and we are told if we worship God we cannot drink whiskey"; while another clinched their objections by saying, "We would have to treat our women as ourselves; and, if we do, then how can we control them?" "But," interposed another, "we should have peace with our neighbours. We have no rest on the top of this rock, nor have we half enough to eat."

So the discussion went on, conducted by the villagers on the one hand, and by the little band of native converts on the other. The old battle between good and evil was again to be fought out on this hill-top. The debate thus begun lasted through the night. As the contestants grew earnest or excited, from time to time, those in the tents, seeking sleep, took anxious note, for they realised how much was at stake. Such as desired Jesus to come and reign over them, an increasing number during the night, together with the native preachers, urged the great benefits that would come to the villagers, if the worship of Yuah should be accepted. The opponents, however, brought forward the arguments, as old as time, against a reformed life. Early in the morning one of the native workers reported that a notable victory for the Lord of glory had been won; and that the whole village had joined in a covenant to receive the worship of Yuah. This consisted in slaying a pig, the flesh of which was divided among all who joined in the covenant. The partaking of the flesh was regarding by them a binding act.

The work of the new life began at once and in earnest. The young man who preached the previous night volunteered to commence evangelistic work immediately. How great a sacrifice this was for him may be judged when it is stated that he was pastor of a prosperous church on the other side of the mountains, where he had a beautiful home. His cheerful change from such a happy environment to this desolation argued well for his loyalty to his Master.

A small bamboo hut was made for him, which was to serve as a dwelling, schoolroom, and chapel. Thus situated, he began his work for the salvation of the village. A school and regular public worship were at once started. It was soon evident, however, that a minority of the villagers would not keep their covenant, or did not intend to do so when they made it, for they drew off. Real Christian converts, however, soon appeared, and after two years' labour the first applicants for baptism presented themselves. Nothing was said to them about a change of dress; yet the new life, begotten in them by the Holy Spirit, was manifested in their earnest desire to be rid of their heathen ornaments, and for a more modest dress. The feeling ran high at this time, and when they determined to take off the wire from their necks and limbs, violence and even death were threatened by the parents of some of the children. But the good life made rapid progress under the devoted ministry of this young man and it was marked by the special power of the Holy Spirit.

After seven years, the missionary party again visited Senite. Reports of the wonderful change that had taken place had reached us from time to time; but we were hardly prepared for the miracle of grace which had been wrought among this people. As we came in view of the former site of the village on the rock, we saw no trace of it. At an expression of our surprise, our guide, the pastor of the church, said, "A little further on you will see the new village." Our advance revealed marvellous changes. In place of the former barbarous and superstitious people, whom we have visited in fear and doubt, we now saw a prosperous Christian community, who united in extending to us a royal welcome. Repeatedly a song broke out from some one in the multitude, which, taken up by others, was echoed back by the overhanging cliffs.

Turning in the path around a projecting mountain spur, we came in sight of the well-ordered and comfortable dwellings of the villagers. They were located on the sloping bank of a sparkling mountain brook, singing its way to the sea. Our mission party stopped and gazed with wonder at the sight before them. Said the missionary to the pastor in charge, "Tee-O, have all the villagers become disciples of Christ?" "No," he replied, "only sixty have joined the church, and last week thirteen more presented themselves for baptism." "What became of the rest?" asked the missionary, recalling the many who made the pledge seven years before. "Most of them remained in the village and have lived a quiet life," answered the pastor, "though they have not yet expressed faith in Christ. A small number of the worst characters have gone away and built a village for themselves. They loved their old life more than the promised blessing," continued Tee-O, "and they went their own way."

The object of this assembling of the Christians was the meeting of the Association of thirty five churches in annual conference, by invitation of the church in Senite. It is impossible to describe the extraordinary jubilation of the native Christians over the wonderful events wrought by our Lord that made it possible to have the meetings at this place.

For two days the church and village entertained nearly seven hundred delegates and visitors. These days were full of the most joyous meetings for business, praise, and prayer. As we entered the village and greeted the bands of glad disciples from far and near, we found the Senite people rejoicing as they welcomed their guests. Their faces were radiant as they crowded around the missionary party with expressions of Thanksgiving and praise, mingled with tears of joy. The difference between the two visits, in the appearance of the people, is beyond description. The horrid heathen ornaments, together with the coils of wire, had disappeared, and neat clothes had taken their place. True, they could not shorten their elongated necks; but scarfs, neatly thrown around the neck, relieved the deformity.

Reaching the place assigned to the missionaries, we found every convenience and comfort at hand which the people could possibly provide. The ground had been swept clean, neat booths had been built, and tables and benches had been conveniently placed; but the crowning feature of the joyful occasion appeared when we saw a great bunch of roses placed on one of the tables for our special enjoyment. How different from the first visit! Yet we saw not so much the beautiful flowers as we did the wonderful transformation in this once savage people. The regenerated men and women crowded about us with overflowing joy in their new life.

Observing a woman who seemed specially happy, we said to her: "Sister, you seem very happy. What is the reason?" "Oh," she replied, "we worship Yuah! When the teacher came to visit us years ago we knew neither Yuah nor the teachers. Whether they had white hearts or black, we could not tell. Now we know that the teachers have white hearts." "But, sister, you have lost the ornaments you used to wear. Do you not miss them?" She replied: "Oh, teacher, we were in bondage then. Now Jesus Christ has set us free; and there is only one woman in the village who will wear the brass wire." Then straightening herself, she exclaimed with emphasis, and not a little disgust; "But she is a heathen." Her appreciation of the awfulness of her former condition could not have been better expressed.

Lifting the roses, we gazed into their wonderful depth of colour, and the prediction of Isaiah seemed fulfilled before us: "The wilderness and the solitary place shall be glad for them; and the desert shall rejoice and blossom as the rose." And there was even more love and Christian fellowship exhibited in this gift when we learned that the rosebushes had been secured a year before for this very occasion by a two days' journey over the mountain. The happy faces about us again declared with increasing emphasis, "The desert shall rejoice and blossom as the rose."

This is the miracle of Senite. Only the power of Divine love could so change the heart of stone into a heart of flesh. Their love for Christ and faith in Him were simple and childlike, such as the Saviour specially commended.

Many young men went from this village to become teachers in other villages. Their schools flourished greatly, and ten years later Senite was still on its upward course, preaching, teaching, and living the Christ-life.

XII - PROVIDENTIAL CARE

Whenever a child of God, pleading for special blessings, receives direct answers from his Heavenly Father, this is indeed a foretaste of heavenly bliss. Such records of God's dealings with His children are so numerous that, were they all recorded in books, the world would not be able to contain them. Happy he who, by stress of discipline, is driven to God for help. And what missionary, relying solely upon God's guidance and deliverance in crises of his experience, has found His ear deaf to his petitions? Experiences illustrating this fact are here recorded.

A few years ago a fire broke out at midnight in the village of Kerway, in the Toungoo hills. It was a large village, having a church of nearly two hundred members. This fire occurred at the close of the dry season, when everything was parched, so that the entire village, including food supplies gathered for the rainy season, was quickly destroyed. The families of five or six native pastors were also involved in this disaster, as they had been left in the village while these pastors were pursuing evangelistic work in neighbouring places. Moreover, as Kerway occupied a central position in the hills, a large supply of school books and medicines had been stored there, and so were lost.

The rainy season in Burma corresponds to winter in the temperate zones, and greatly restricts travel and labour. So our situation was made more trying. Our plans for school work had been frustrated, and our evangelistic work was greatly impeded. Such a calamity threw a gloom over the whole mission; and the more so as its resources for the year had already been exhausted. How this necessity could be met was a problem we could not solve. In a few days teacher Kah Baw, the pastor of the church, with a delegation of its members, appeared at the missionary headquarters in Toungoo. They were half-clad, for they had escaped from the fire with only the clothes they had on, and having lost everything, they were greatly depressed. They seated themselves on the floor, and, looking up into the face of their missionary, Kah Baw said: "Teacher, we have lost everything. Not even a Bible or hymn-book is left. What shall we do?" Then he added: "My children, who live in a neighbouring village, have asked me to come to them, promising to give me food and clothes. But," added the dear old man, without the least thought he was doing a heroic act, "I cannot leave my people. The worship of God will be destroyed in my village, if I leave. I shall build me a little bamboo hut, and give them what strength and care I can. But, teacher, can you help us?"

The teacher replied: "There is no money in the treasury, and already, to meet the needs of our evangelists, all the money we dare borrow has been advanced. We have therefore, dear brothers, no other source of help than our God. But He is sufficient." Many times we have bowed in prayer with Kah Baw in days past, when working together in building up this great mission: and so we began to rehearse these deliverances for the encouragement of this disheartened band. "Yes," replied Kah Baw, "the God of Abraham, Issac, and Jacob, who never failed His ancient people, has certainly never failed us. We will take our case to Him."

So we all bowed in prayer to God. The native Christians, as usual, prostrated themselves with their faces on the floor, and their petitions were remarkable for their simplicity and trust. They were like little children pleading with their loving father. This is characteristic of converts from heathenism. We felt completely dependent upon God's providential help, the most blessed necessity into which a child of God can come. There were few dry eyes in the little company when we arose from our knees. "Now, brothers," said the teacher, "we must wait for God's answer."

La Quai, Karen Evangelist

A Buddhist Pongyi

A small sum was given to Kah Baw to purchase rice; for they had fasted a long time. A weekly foreign mail was expected to reach Toungoo in two days. We were confidently looking for help in answer to our prayers, and thought it might come from America; though it was not the season to expect help from this source. In two days the mail from America arrived, and was unusually large. The first question suggested to us was, "Has God sent us help?" The very first letter we opened disclosed a bright German stater. It came from an old school friend, from whom we had not heard for years. This glad surprise, which should not have been a surprise to unfaltering faith, may be understood by some, though difficult to describe. It was as if a voice from heaven had said, "O thou of little faith, wherefore didst thou doubt?" Old Kah Baw and his friends were summoned; but before they reached us another letter was found containing a check for ten pounds, sent by a life-long helper in Providence, R. I. "There," said the teacher to Kah Baw, "is God's answer to our prayers; enough to supply you and the other five teachers with food for the rains, and also Bibles, hymn-books, and necessary clothes. Let us thank God for His gifts."

There was a clear note of joy and victory in their Thanksgiving. It is safe to say that Kah Baw and his followers, and as many as heard of this wonderful answer, and were partakers of its blessing, were confirmed believers in prayer to Yuah, and of His faithfulness as a prayer-hearing and prayer-answering God.

The next mail brought another check for twelve additional pounds to meet any "incidental needs." And the strange thing about it was that the donors of these gifts had sent them under the strong impression that God was directing them in their offerings.

But answers to prayer are not always as direct as in the above instance. God often veils Himself in His providences, so that His answers to prayer are at times hidden, and may not be realised by the petitioner until the lapse of years. An experience came to us in our early missionary life which illustrates this fact.

Our mission station was then located about a mile from the town of Toungoo in the jungle. We were beyond police protection, and had no white neighbours nearer than the town. Only the school children and frequent Karen visitors were with us. Robbers, called dacoits in Burma, were roaming about the country, singly and in companies, and were merciless in their deeds of violence. We had bestowed only a passing thought on these perils. We bowed in prayer morning and evening, committing the care of ourselves and our mission to our Heavenly Father. We had firearms in the house, but had no thought of using them for defence. Our youngest child was about six months old, and she had formed the habit of awaking about one or two o'clock at night for a drink of water. So habitual was this that her mother was accustomed to place a glass of water on a stand by her bed. The servant was also requested to fill the earthen cooler on the sideboard every day, and this he usually did. On the night in question the child awoke as usual, but by some oversight the glass of water was absent. I was asked to go to the cooler on the sideboard to supply the lack. There also I found no water. This was a surprise, and necessitated my going around the house on the veranda (we lived on the second story) to a filter. It was light enough to see clearly all objects near at hand. At the back of the house all ell projected, which was used for a bathroom. All the windows of the house were protected by wooden shutters, which we carefully barred at night.

As I stooped to dip water from the filter, I happened (if anything happens by chance) to look across to the window in the ell, which I had barred that night. There I saw a Burman stark naked, hanging across the window-sill, with knife in hand, on the point of entering. He had pried open the window in some way, and the whole house was open to his will. It was, of course, impossible to know how many accomplices he might have. There was nothing to hinder him and his fellows, if he had any, from reaching every room in the house. Only this discovery at the crucial moment, occasioned by the circumstances above narrated, enabled us to defend our house and family.

This providential interposition in our behalf made a strong impression upon our hearts in all subsequent years. If it can be proved that God watches over His children carefully at all times, what rest should come to the faith of those who trust in Him! We could not, in considering the events of that night, doubt that a loving intelligence had truly interposed for our protection. If we were to consider the doctrine of chances, there could not have been, in our conception, a combination of chance events to provide such definite results.

Here are the events that combined to give us the necessary warning. First, the awakening of the little child at the fixed time; second, the forgetting to place the water on the stand as usual; third, the failure of the servant to put water into the cooler, and hence the necessity of going to the filter on the back veranda; and these all so timed as to bring me to the danger-spot just when needed. A minute earlier or later, and the robber would not have been discovered. Such a combination of events argued beyond reasonable doubt that a wise and benevolent mind had our welfare in charge. God does not vacillate or change, like men, in His treatment of His children. One clear case like the above guarantees His constant care. So we felt, and thus was our faith confirmed for days to come. One can realise with what gratitude we rested in the care of the loving Father ever after. Many can recall like providences in their lives. The foot-steps of God are discerned only by the eye of faith; and how blessed is he who learns how to trace them.

The outcome of this adventure also shows God's interposition. I looked for some weapon to attack the robber, as he was balanced on the window-sill, but even the brick, which had been for months beside the filter, had been removed, and nothing else presented itself. Seeing that the robber had become alarmed, I called to my wife in English, to bring my rifle, which stood at the head of my bed. She replied that she could not find it. In cleaning it, I had changed its position. Thus was I kept from shedding human blood. I then darted back through the house, finding my gun on the way. Passing through the rear door, I fired into the air to convince any armed men that we were prepared for defence. The robber escaped, and we were left unharmed. Though we continued to live in the same place for many years, this was the only attempt at robbery that we experienced.

Such manifest interpositions of God afford His devout children encouragement and trust beyond human estimate. These are experiences to be carefully treasured for help in the future battles of faith.

A very notable experience of this kind comes to mind at this point worthy of record. The rainy season had passed, and the travelling season had arrived. There was great need that year for travel, since among the score of churches under the missionary's care there were some that sadly needed discipline. It cannot be expected that the best of churches organised from recent converts from heathenism will be better or more advanced than the average church in America. Divisions and misunderstandings will arise even in the home churches. How much more are they to be anticipated in a new mission field. These divisions were a heavy burden on the heart of the missionary, and he hastened his tour of investigation. His bearers had assembled at his home, from the mountains, goods were packed in their baskets, and all was ready for a start in the morning. That night our little girl fell ill with a severe fever; and, being no better in the morning, how could we leave her for a month or more, carrying with us this additional load of anxiety?

So I decided to send on the bearers, while I waited for a favourable change in the health of the child. In a day or so she had so much improved that we set out for the mountains, taking with us three Karens and two saddle-ponies. I led the party through the thick jungle grass, which covered the whole plain, to the mountains, twenty miles distant. The jungle-path which we followed through the grass had been the haunt, through the rains, of a man-eating tiger, which was said to have killed more than a score of native people. These tigers are peculiarly fierce; for, having lost their claws and teeth from old age, they are no longer able to pull down the jungle animals that form their usual food. They, therefore, beset some jungle trail and prey on human beings, whom they easily capture. Being full of care and anxiety about the sick child I had left, and also about the state of my churches, I quite forgot the tiger, and tramped alone ahead of my attendants. After travelling six or eight miles through the dense grass, which was eight or ten feet in height, I came to a jungle stream flowing across the path. As I approached the bank a hornbill arose from the bushes on the opposite side and flew into the top of a small tree. This surprised me, as the bird is seldom seen save on the highest trees. As the Karens are specially fond of its flesh, I shot the bird. And that shot not only killed the bird, but apparently saved my own life, for the tiger had been stalking me through the jungle, as a cat does a mouse, seeking a good chance to pounce upon me. This he certainly would have had at this ford. I heard his leaps into the jungle very near me; and the ponies, scenting the beast, as they are quick to do, were so frightened, together with the three Karens who were leading them, that the latter began to shout to me: "Oh, teacher, we are all dead men, for there is a tiger about! The ponies will break away from us!" I shouted back "The tiger has gone! Fear not! Come on! Surely God has delivered us!"

We crossed the brook, and joyfully continued our journey. The manifest interposition of God in our behalf had taught us to put our trust implicitly in Him. And we felt rebuked, as well as comforted; for God, who could so easily protect us from the wild beast, could as easily heal our little child and care for the churches which Christ had bought with His own blood.

XIII - THE MAGIC DOUGHNUT

For those who have eyes to see there are many beautiful flowers in the Lord's spiritual garden. These are often found in obscure and unexpected places among men, but always bear the mark of their heavenly origin. What rose or pink can match the marvellous beauty of Divine love, or self-denial, or thoughtfulness for others' good? Their fragrance is sweeter far than that of the most fragrant orchid of the tropics; and when we suddenly come within their range, our souls are delighted, and we give thanks.

One travelling season in the Burman mountains, while on a tour among the churches, I came to a large village on a mountain-top, and, having completed my inspection of the church and school, I retired to my tent for the night. A feeling of loneliness came over me, caused, it may be, by long absence from my native land and weeks of separation from the society of our mission headquarters. For relief, I settled down to read, when some one outside the tent-door began calling "Tharah! Tharah!" which means "Teacher! Teacher!"

With a slight impatience I laid down my book, thinking it to be another application for medicine, and opened the tent-door. There stood a Karen woman with a large lacquered tray, on which was placed what seemed to me, in such a place, almost a miracle. When one is told that there was not an ounce of wheat flour in all those mountains, he may be able to share my surprise at seeing a tray of New England doughnuts, having the right colour and shape, and the regulation hole in the centre.

Questioning the woman, I found that, when she learned of the coming of the missionary, her kind and thoughtful Christian heart moved her to prepare a glad surprise for him. She had spent the previous afternoon in pounding rice in a wooden mortar and sifting it through a piece of gauze, to obtain rice flour for the coveted doughnuts. She fashioned them into the required form, and cooked them in lard. "But," I asked, "how did you know how to make them?" "Oh," she replied, "years ago, when at school in the city, I used to help the Mama about her cooking, and sometimes, when another missionary would visit her, she would make these strange cakes, and the visitors always seemed very happy to see them. I thought they must have some magic about them, so when I heard that you were coming to our village, I planned to make some to surprise you."

Then we understood the magic of the cakes. For occasionally, when missionaries met for a brief season, they endeavoured to secure some article of food which would bring back memories of earlier home-days, and this often took the form of the New England doughnut.

No heathen woman would thus have remembered us. It was as the ripe fruit of the Spirit of Christ, or a flower from the heavenly garden, blooming on the hill-top among the Toungoo jungles. It is true, when we came to sample the cakes, that they were hard and indigestible; but, being mixed with Christian love, nothing could have delighted the palate more than these. They proved truly to be the "magic doughnut."

XIV - A NOTABLE MISSIONARY JOURNEY

In the cold season of 1882, it was decided in family counsel that we all should attend the annual Association. The two women missionaries of the station were also to accompany us. Our party numbered six, including our two girls of eight and five years respectively. Some of the native school children also accompanied us. The plan was to spend two months on the mountains among the churches, and also to make an extended tour among the heathen Brecs. This was no slight understanding; for it involved travelling over broad plains and up steep, rugged mountains, with the fording of rapid mountain streams. The problem was how to transport the little folks, and how to take supplies for so long a journey. We would need everything in the line of food, except chickens, eggs, and rice. These we could obtain along our way. We would also need to take clothing and bedding, and medicines for the sick. For transportation we had the native pony, a hardy beast, small but strong, and well adapted for such a journey. We also had twenty-nine native bearers to carry the goods.

During the first days of the new year our twenty-nine packs were ready for the bearers, and by eleven o'clock on Friday morning we had crossed the river and entered the great forest. Thus began one of the most momentous jungle tours in our missionary life of forty years.

The first night found us ten miles on our journey, and encamped in a beautiful grove of bamboos by a stream of clear, running water. It was a charming, moonlight evening, and our company was buoyant in spirit, including the school children, just freed from their year's confinement at study. As we had few cooking utensils, the preparation of food was carried on by the native disciples through the night. The hum of conversation, with the stirring about of the busy natives, disturbed our sleep, yet before sunrise we were again on the march.

At first the little girls were carried in woven bamboo hammocks, made by the natives. When the way became steep and crooked, these were discarded, and the native pastors carried the children on their backs, much to the little girls' delight. Their carriers also pleased them by climbing trees to get beautiful and fragrant orchids for them. But the greater part of the journey was made by the little folks on foot.

Our second days' journey was through dense forests, along the bed of a mountain stream. Tropical plants everywhere abounded, and with these were some that we have loved in the homeland; while over all towered the majestic forest trees, interlaced with large creepers, whose flowering festoons lent a unique charm to our journey. Before night we had crossed the first range of mountains and reached a Christian village, where we prepared to spend the Lord's Day. A plat of ground had been cleared by the native disciples for our tent. They had also provided wood, water, and everything possible for our comfort.

Monday morning we were off again for the Association. Between us and the Association grounds lay a deep gulf, at the bottom of which ran a swift mountain stream. This stream for untold ages had been cutting its way through the mountain ranges, in some places to a depth of more than a thousand feet. In some places it could not be forded, and suspension bridges of swinging or floating bamboo had been made for the accommodation of travellers. We reached the edge of this deep gulf about nine o'clock in the morning; and, while making the descent, we observed above the river another river of fog, which seemed to be flowing parallel with it. Penetrating this, we quickly passed out of the bright sunshine into twilight. The women of the party found much discomfort in walking through the jungle bushes, drenched with the mist, and on reaching the river at the bottom of the gulf, all were in a bedraggled condition.

A narrow, floating bridge had been made for our crossing. It would support only two at a time, and even then sank several inches, requiring some nerve to cross it in safety. But we all went over barefooted, shoes in hand and heart in mouth. The sun at last having dissipated the fog, we began the steep ascent. For this work the mountain ponies and barefooted Karens were admirably fitted. That night we reached the Association grounds and went into camp.

Heathen Visitors, Mountain Karens

Early the following day the clans began to gather; and, as we stood on the elevated ground occupied by our camp, the scene about us was most inspiring. Groups of delegates and school children in their bright holiday dress were coming from every quarter to the camp. As the companies wound round the hill-tops, and over the mountain ridges through the forests of bamboos, all intent upon the service of the one blessed Lord, our hearts were filled with gratitude and praise. The scene was well calculated to suggest those happy days in the history of God's ancient people, when from every quarter of their holy land they wended their way to Jerusalem to observe the annual feast of the passover, and, reaching the hill-tops overlooking the sacred city with its magnificent temple, their voices broke forth in jubilant songs of praise to the great Jehovah.

The exercises occupied two days, including the regular business of the Association, interspersed with gospel songs by the numerous schools that were represented. And all this took place in a country only a few years before swept by tribal wars and the horrible practices of heathenism.

The site of the Association was on the range of mountains next to the watershed. This range towered thousands of feet above us, yet seemed very near. As we stood looking over the scene, there suddenly burst upon our ears the report of guns and the discordant beating of drums. All the villagers rushed forward to see what this might mean. We saw approaching in the distance a large band of armed men. They were coming from the land of the dreaded Brecs. Immediately fear fell upon the assembled host; for, said they, "These men are coming to fulfil their threat to break up our meetings."

Meanwhile, the Brecs were rapidly approaching, their discordant music echoing among the hills. Their leaders were known to our native missionaries, and were quickly introduced to us. The chief was a giant, and looked to be anything but a savage. His name was Howee (The "Blessed"). We welcomed them so cordially that they soon appeared to feel quite at home, and declared they had come to secure teachers of the "new religion" for their people. The change of feeling among the assembled clans, on hearing this good news, was very great. The gong sounded for the assembling of the people, and the service became one of earnest praise for this direct answer to their prayers, for God had given them an open door into this savage tribe. Howee and his wild men watched the proceedings with intense interest, and later he declared that, if the white missionaries would visit his people, he believed they would turn to the worship of the living God.

Our mission party subsequently determined to divide. One part was to travel on the western side of the watershed, while the other would follow the lead of Howee and his savage band back to their country. This was a great undertaking, for that towering range of mountains before us must be crossed, and what awaited us beyond them none could foretell.

From our camp the distance to the foot of the high range seemed short; yet it required two days' march to reach it. We were now in a very wild country, seldom, if ever, traversed by a white man. We were told that the road up the mountain was impossible to ascend; but an intelligent Karen preceded us and cut a passable path around the obstacles, while our nimble bearers climbed the face of the almost impassable cliff to the road beyond. We camped at night, after passing the first difficulties of the journey, on a narrow ridge, with the giant forests about us, while above the tree-tops towered the mountains we must yet cross. Our party consisted of the missionary, his wife and children, and native evangelists, led by Howee and more than thirty of his men, besides a throng of savages from the surrounding villages, attracted by curiosity.

Our native Christians had built bonfires, which we found very acceptable in the crisp evening air. The cook and the natives were soon all busy preparing the evening meal. Later all the company gathered for a meeting of prayer and praise, at which many of the savages heard the gospel for the first time. They could not grasp its meaning, yet showed an attentive and friendly spirit. Then followed a season of conversation between the missionaries and the natives, in which many questions were asked and answered. This was followed on the part of the natives by an exhibition of their skill in throwing the spear, in which they greatly excelled. We in turn showed them an unloaded revolver, which excited their wonder. When told it was a weapon for shooting, some handled it with undisguised contempt, seemingly thinking that so small a thing was not to be feared. But when we slipped several cartridges into place, selected a mark in a safe position, and rapidly discharged the "baby gun," their astonishment was beyond description. The loudness of the report and the effect of so small a gun upon the mark were so great that the more savage among them were ready to fall down and worship it. It served as a good warning for those who were unfriendly or disposed to look with greed upon our luggage, which was to them of untold wealth. In all our future journeyings on this tour, though often separated from our luggage, which was carried by these same or similar savages, nothing was lost.

The night was spent by the native preachers telling the story of the cross, and in answering numerous questions asked by the wild men camping with us. Two o'clock found all the natives astir, cooking their breakfast in order to make an early start for the next mountain's climb. Our camp being a little removed from the main encampment, refreshing sleep was secured till the morning star appeared. Then we awoke, and, after breakfast in the early dawn under the trees, we started on our day's journey. Our large company, in single file, now began the hardest climb of the trip. The mountain was so steep in places that we were obliged to use both hands and feet in making the ascent. As no water could be secured along the way, all had provided themselves with bamboo bottles filled with water and food. Looking back at our large company winding in and out among the trees, it presented an impressive scene. The sun was just shooting its yellow rays across the landscape, the air was crisp and invigorating, and the Christians of our party, full of good cheer, caused the mountain-tops to echo with their hymns of praise; while the heathen of the company, bearing their heavy loads, tramped silently and stolidly on and up. During the ascent we were often obliged to stop for a rest, and how like a beautiful dream the landscape below unrolled before us. Each stop brought out new and wonderful views.

By eleven o'clock we drew near the top of the range, and what we had thought to be rock proved to be brown grass, which the frost had killed. Stunted trees grew to the very crown of the range, and to our New England eyes took the form of an orchard of apple-trees. We were soon among them, and found ourselves in the habitat of a great variety of choice orchids. The air was loaded with their sweetness. Our school-boys cast down their burdens, and were soon climbing the trees and gathering armfuls of these wonders of the tropics. Our little girls for once had all the flowers they could desire; and as each boy brought in his contribution and cast it down at their feet, they were almost covered with the blossoms.

We were now near the summit. One more climb and the long company filed out upon the ridge of the mountain. We had agreed not to look back until the top was reached; and here, upon a rock floor over six thousand feet above the sea, we gazed with bewildered delight upon the most magnificent mountain scenery we had ever beheld.

Looking westward, over our long pathway, we were first attracted by the four ranges running north and south, over which we had so laboriously climbed. The farthest range, almost absorbed in the distant blue, marked the line between the mountain system and the plains of Toungoo. The mountains were broken into sharp peaks and cragged precipices, and yet they were beautifully symmetrical in their disorder. The line marking the river we had crossed, and its gulf, stretched from extreme north to extreme south, and looked like a ribbon of burnished silver where the waters reflected the sunlight.

Some one has said, "How like a cauldron of violently boiling water suddenly congealed, the mountain ranges appear." The truth of this simile was there impressed upon me. As we gazed, new surprises sprang up from every quarter. Trees near at hand covered with brilliant flowers, and the shadows from clouds floating across the landscape in swift flight, gave us a scene of surpassing beauty. The calls of baboons, sounding like a company of boys just out of school, the chatter of monkeys in the distant groves, the screaming of flocks of bright paraquets, the call of strange birds, and the hum of bees surrounded us. A more careful observation of the plants and trees in the immediate neighbourhood moved us to almost tearful delight as we discovered grasses, poverty weed, motherwort, wandering Jew, everlasting, and bright patches of red coxcomb, all of which we knew in the dear home-land. Then there was a variety of tropical trees and plants, including the giant fern, the dwarf palms, their feathery leaves loaded with seeds, and the wild gooseberry of the tropics growing on trees ten to fifteen feet in height.

Native Carriers with Missionary Outfit

As we stood contemplating these physical wonders we recalled the fact that this vast mountain region, only a few years before, was filled with the gloom of absolute savagery–village at war with village, and clan with clan, the hills resounding with the confusion of battle and the discordant cries of heathen. But now, while gazing on the enchanting scene, we could justly add to it the glory of a redeemed land. Within the sphere of our vision there were now seventy-five fully organised churches of Christ, fifty schools filled with boys and girls of vigorous minds and a consuming thirst for knowledge, and ninety-one teachers, ordained and un-ordained, ministering to these churches, and preaching among the villages yet in heathenism. The little brown spots in the vivid green of the forests, and the columns of smoke in the distant blue, marked the sites of these villages. How many journeys filled with anxiety had been made back and forth among these mountain ranges in the past. Standing on our high lookout, with supreme exultation in the love and power of Christ to save the lost, we girded ourselves anew to look upon the dark scenes in the east; for, in a certain sense, this mountain range marked the boundary between the past years of conquest and the victories yet to be won for our Prince Emmanuel.

Then looking eastward we saw a duplicate view of the western prospect, yet in many respects dissimilar. There was the same view of mountains, though these were more precipitous, range beyond range of north and south trend, vanishing in the far horizon. We had, however, reached a semi-tropical climate. There were groves of stately pines, and even at our feet stood a friend from our home-land–the graceful birch, fraternising with the bamboo. But we knew that the brown spots in the vivid green no longer marked places where God was worshipped. No white missionary had ever visited this field. Very few native pastors had ventured into this country. Only Soo Thah and his companions had passed over the road, and preached the gospel in any village. As a result of Soo Thah's work we were on our journey, at the invitation of Howee, to visit the heart of the country now spread out before us. How gloomy and dark it appeared to us in contrast with the western side. The same sun was shining brightly upon these ragged mountain peaks, but not a single disciple of Christ was there. Neither chapel nor school, harbingers of a Christian civilisation, had yet been established in all this region.

In our meditations at that hour, there came to us the inspiring words of Isaiah, "How beautiful upon the mountains are the feet of him that bringeth good tidings, that publisheth peace; that bringeth good tidings of good, that publisheth salvation"; and our hearts were cheered by the prospect presented to our faith, that we should see the time in the near future when these mountains would break forth in songs of praise to the great Redeemer.

Gathering up our baggage, we started down the eastern side of the mountain. We were now on the border of Howee's country, the land of the dreaded Brecs; and what was our surprise to find, instead of tangled paths, a broad road cleared for us of all underbrush. And in many places these dear heathen had swept the road clear of twigs and leaves. This token of kind reception put our party in the best of spirits, and the little girls scampered down the mountain like lambs at play, and the disciples broke forth in hymns of praise. We found too, that these thoughtful heathen had brought bamboo buckets of clear, cool water from some spring, and had put them in convenient places for our refreshment. Then further down we came upon bamboo buckets filled with steaming rice, which the young heathen women had prepared for the party.

Coming out in a little opening of the pines, we saw the village of our quest, nestling in the curve of a precipitous hill, rising before us. It was apparently nearby, yet for two hours or more we tramped steadily on, so crooked was the road, winding in and out among the hills. Passing round a projecting spur, we came suddenly upon the village; yet not unexpectedly, for we had noticed runners at different points, who suddenly disappeared, doubtless to announce our approach. Our appearance was a signal for an outbreak of intense excitement. Few of the people had ever seen a white person, or even a pony. They seemed to think that the riders were a part of the ponies! Some screamed out in terror, and others were too frightened to flee.

Some women were dipping water from the brook we had to cross, and one old mother, who had just filled her bucket with water, pounded it upon the ground, exclaiming, "Ah-wee! Ah-wee"–an expression of supreme surprise. Soon our company had dismounted, and, the first fright of the people having passed, we all began making friends. They had heard something about shaking hands, as a sign of fellowship; so some, observing the handshaking, approached with the offer of their own hands. The amphitheatre was crowded with houses, leaving no space for pitching our tent; so a shelf on the rocks above the village was prepared for this purpose.

We tarried among this people for a week, preaching the good news and seeking to persuade them to turn from their heathen practices to the worship and service of the true God. They were apparently tired and sick of the lives they had been leading, and were especially groaning under their galling bondage to the "nats," or evil spirits, which they imagined were swarming about them, and ever seeking their ruin. For this cause they seemed the more willing to consider our message and follow our counsels. As the particulars of this missionary work are given in our book, "Soo Thah," we will not repeat them here. Suffice it to say that the people generally turned away from their old superstitions and honestly sought to walk in the Christian way, as their evangelist teachers should guide them.

Thus were we led to hope that the gospel of Christ would win its way among these wild people, who had been the terror of our adjoining mission outposts; and this hope did not fail of blessed fruition.

At the time of our departure the natives crowded about us in the best of feeling to shake hands; for they said, "We are all now in the worship of Jehovah, and we are so glad." They showed their gladness by their happy looks and hearty handshakes. We parted, with their joyous cries in our ears: "Now we worship Jehovah! Now we worship Jehovah!" And so we filed away down the path on our day's journey.

During the next two or three weeks, we were constantly travelling from village to village through some of the grandest mountain scenery. Our course took us back among the disciples on the watershed range, and our time was spent in strengthening weak churches, and in founding new interests. The delight of the rich scenery and the fragrant pine woods through which we passed far outweighed all weariness and gave us constant joy.

And yet our pleasures were not without some annoying interruptions. For instance, one day, after climbing a very steep mountain, we came to a deserted village. Our followers had gone ahead with the little girls, while we followed. Stopping a moment to look at the spot occupied by the village, we were suddenly attacked by myriads of fleas, which drove us to a precipitous flight. This revealed the reason why the Karens often desert their villages. The ever-increasing vermin drive them to new localities. The ground of this deserted village was so covered with the fleas that it took their colour.

Our remaining journey for the day was through a dense jungle up the mountain-side and along its towering ridge, from which we caught wonderful views on either side. At night we camped on the top of the range at the head of a deep ravine that ran down to the foot of the mountain. It had been threatening rain all the afternoon, and now from our encampment, where the sun was shining brightly, we looked down upon the black clouds, heaving like a ragging sea, while through them darted shafts of blinding lightning. As the clouds were slowly rising towards us, no little uneasiness was felt about the possible effect of the tempest. Tent ropes were tightened, and ditches dug around our tents.

The natives had cut paths into the high grass, and prepared neat shelters for dry weather, but they were no protection against a rainstorm. When the night began to shut in the clouds swept upwards like the rushing charge of an army, the main part, however, passing up a neighbouring ravine, much to our relief. Yet a part of the tempest struck our encampment. The downpour of rain, mingled with the roar of the wind and the reverberation of the thunder claps from the surrounding mountain-peaks, was almost terrifying in its grandeur. Our natives could hardly be expected to appreciate this grandeur, as their frail shelters were torn down by the wind, and the rain deluged them. The cook had prepared a nice shelter for his pots and kettles, which the wind scattered, and his dumb wife, greatly frightened, added to the general confusion by her efforts to express her dismay. This caused much merriment among the people. The storm passed as speedily as it had risen, but the memory of the thunder reverberating among the mountain-tops remained with us a long time.

The next morning we arose early, much refreshed, and ready for our northward journey. It was along the boundary between the English territory and the independent tribes to the eastward. The travelling was hard, yet relieved by the grandeur of the scenery. After several days' journeying amid the marvels of nature, we reached the extreme northern limit of our mission field–Yahdo valley, which we have already described. The change from mountain travel to that of the broad, open pathway of the valley was grateful to us all.

On our arrival in Yahdo, the numerous Christians extended to us a very hearty greeting. Many willing hands made the work of pitching our tents easy, and we were soon at rest. How delightful, after spending so long a time among the unsympathising heathen, to enjoy the close and warm fellowship of our Christian brethren. Here we spent a week of strenuous work. We found five candidates for baptism awaiting our arrival. On Saturday their examination took place, and the baptism was appointed for the morrow. The news spread quickly through the surrounding villages that a baptism among the Christians was to take place.

So early Sunday morning people began to gather from all quarters to the appointed place. This was a beautiful, clear pool in the mountain stream, overshadowed by willows. The sun shone brightly, and all nature seemed at peace. Yet what a strange company had gathered to witness this Christian ordinance–for the most part savages, wild-eyed, armed with spears and swords. They said, among themselves, that the teacher was going to put some men and women under the water to see "Yuah." Where they got this idea no one could tell. The five candidates, three of them women, stood beside the pool. The young men and women of the church stood near, hymn-books in hand. The missionary also was there. The Holy Spirit seemed to overshadow the little assembly of disciples, and all felt His presence. The multitude of heathen also seemed to be under some spell, for they ceased their conversation, and the whole company appeared reverent. One of the candidates had waited two years for baptism, hoping that his wife would join him in this public confession of faith in Christ. She now stood by his side for this purpose, and his happiness was complete. The simple Scriptural ceremony of burial with Christ and resurrection to newness of life, with the accompaniment of prayer and singing, was vastly more impressive than when observed in the most stately sanctuary. The native pastor administered the baptism, the benediction was pronounced, and the vast and strangely constituted assembly scattered without confusion to their homes.

In the afternoon the right hand of fellowship was given to the new members of the church, and the Lord's Supper observed. Monday and Tuesday, meetings were held in the interests of the mission, and everything was set in order. Wednesday we turned homeward for the City of Toungoo. After five days of wearisome travel, we reached our own home again. The journey of two months had been made largely on foot, even by the little girls. No happier missionary tour could have been devised and experienced, and, in view of the amount of work accomplished, it would hardly have been more useful. We could but recognise in it the good hand of our God, and we ascribed to Him all the glory.

XV - THE GOSPEL AND THE SAVAGE BRECS

This people, as shown in the previous chapter, were located beyond the great range of mountains which form the eastern watershed, and also the boundary between English territory and the independent tribes. On the western side of this watershed the gospel had been introduced and churches established. In 1865, when we entered this mission field, there were nine organised churches. Hundreds of villages were yet groping in heathen darkness. But year by year the gospel extended its peaceful conquests, until this highest mountain barrier was reached.

Oftentimes the missionary, amidst his slow conquests, would cast wistful eyes to the distant, mysterious east, wondering what kind of people dwelt there. It was to him a terra incognita. Frequent raids were made by these savages into the English territory, burning villages and slaughtering the inhabitants; but little was known of these hostile people, save that they were reported to be exceedingly savage and cruel. This fact was clearly shown by their murderous raids.

In course of time the conquests of the gospel among the eastern mountains had pushed the line of light up to the borders of this unknown land. Often the native pastors and evangelists considered the question of visiting this land. But the reports of the savage cruelties of the Brecs were rehearsed as a serious objection to any attempt to evangelise them. There were many reports of traders who had visited the country and never returned; and of others who had returned stripped of everything, even to their clothes. To enter such a territory, it was urged, would be to challenge death. Spies had been sent into the land to discover if evangelists could safely enter, but they brought no encouragement. However, the interest in these tribes among the native Christians was steadily increasing.

At last, in one of the annual meetings of the churches, the question of a mission to the Brec Karens was brought forward and earnestly discussed. It was easy to see that something ought to be done for these savage people, but by what agency it was difficult to determine. Finally it was decided that it must be undertaken as in apostolic times. Accordingly, volunteers were sought to go across the mountains.

Young men were soon found who were willing to attempt this hazardous work. Their reception in the Brec country was at first most hostile. They were accused of being spies, and were surrounded by armed and threatening men. But, filled with apostolic zeal and courage, they overcame all opposition by the book they carried (the "white book" in the traditions of the people), and by their sweet singing. Thus hostility was changed into a friendly greeting.

The settlement into which these messengers entered was one of the most savage in the whole Brec country. It consisted of a series of villages located in a broad amphitheatre, formed by horseshoe-curved cliffs three or four hundred feet in height, thus making a natural stronghold. Here the first messengers of the gospel were received, and the confidence of the people won. In succeeding years other young men joined this mission, and a small school was begun. The difficulties that confronted them in this pioneer work are indescribable. But the declaration of the gospel–the love of God, the coming of His Son, His life, teaching, sacrificial death, and resurrection–applied to the hearts of the people by the Holy Spirit, gradually wrought its work here as elsewhere, bringing souls to repentance and to the beginning of a new life.

On the first visit of a white missionary, the villagers assembled and asked him to destroy for them their symbols of heathen worship. This was a great step, and marked their sincerity in asking for a teacher to tell them of Yuah. At first it seemed as if the whole village had turned to God; but it was far otherwise. Yet never was the Spirit's work in connection with the preaching of the gospel made more manifest. One might expect that the more intelligent would first show signs of a new life; but it was not uncommon for the less intelligent among them to be first in giving abiding evidence that they had truly passed from death into life.

The reformation of this village was slow, and only as the people grasped the idea that God's son had come to earth, and borne their sins upon the cross. They readily understood the substitution of the innocent for the guilty, and humbly accepted Christ's redemptive work in their behalf. This thought wrought mightily in the hearts of even the most simple-minded, in awakening love to Christ as an incentive to right living. Nor was this reformation confined, in its effects, to those who came to trust in Christ. It changed the life of the whole village, and seemed to awaken in the hearts of all a new sense of propriety and of upright living.

From the first, even among the most degraded, there seemed to be a clear sense of the principles of right and wrong. We never needed to convince them of personal sin and guilt. They recognised these facts, and, because of them, they declared that "Yuah had forsaken them." To them the good news was the declaration of a new fact: namely, that Jesus Christ came to save them from their sins, and to make it possible, through their repentance and trust in Him, to become the sons of God. These truths were ever foremost in our dealing with these savage races. Other villages saw the prosperity which had come to this leading village, after they had adopted the worship of God, and so called for teachers that they might follow in this way.

An incident that added vitally in leading the people to this change occurred most fortunately at a time when it would accomplish most for the good cause. One of the most prominent of the Brec chiefs, Tee Peh, with a large body of his followers, stood out in opposition to the regeneration of his tribe; and after a number of years; when several villages had become settled in their new worship, his opposition broke out into open violence. There being no law among these tribes, the weak were unprotected. From the beginning of the preaching of the gospel among these villages, the return of "Yuah" (the God of their traditions), to a beneficent care of His children, had been prominent in the faith of the new disciples.

A council was held at Tee Peh's village to consider the question of an attack upon the Christian villages. Tee Peh and his followers, who were suffering from pressure of famine, seeing Christian villages well supplied with food, became envious of their prosperity. Having heard that the Yuah of the Christians had returned to them, and had made them the object of His care, they were doubtful of the success of such an attack. Some of his people opposed, on the ground that Yuah was a living God and lived among His children, and that their prosperity proved this. Tee Peh, however, urged that they did not really know that Yuah was a living God till they should put Him to proof. Like the cunning old heathen that he was, he proposed that a test case be made. They would make a raid upon a Christian village, seize some of the children, if possible, and hold them for ransom. If Yuah came for them, they would deliver them up, and so escape punishment; if He did not come, they would know surely that Yuah was like the dead gods of the Burmans, and they would then have nothing to fear from Him.

The majority of Tee Peh's followers were enthusiastic over this plan of their leader, and were ready to execute it. The Christians, having heard of this council, and the plans of Tee Peh, were filled with alarm. Their faith, yet in its infancy, was small in proportion to the crisis presented to them. Their teachers consulted over the situation with the missionary, and were urged to meet the test with prayer and faith. Examples of conquering faith in similar circumstances in the Old Testament times were freely discussed.

During the following rainy season, Tee Peh, with a band of his followers, carried out his threat. He attacked one of the Christian villages and got away with two captive children. Runners came at once to the mission headquarters, in the city of Toungoo, with letters informing us of what had occurred. We saw that the old chief had thrown down the gage of battle to the Christians in his tribe, and that they must take it up, or acknowledge a defeat. Such a defeat filled us with dread. It would stop all further advance of spiritual work among the Brec tribe, if it did not break up the churches already gathered. It would strengthen doubt among the many churches on the west side of the watershed and paralyse the work of the anti-evangelists in the whole field.

This was clearly a spiritual warfare. The native Christians so regarded it. It was clear that we could not oppose force with force; nor was there any possible help save in the almighty power of Jehovah Jireh, the God of missions. We took the letter into our private room, and spread it before the Lord of glory, and appealed to Him for help. He gave to us a satisfying assurance of gracious succour.

Letters were sent to the churches, the case plainly stated, and prayer asked. The elders and devout men were summoned to meet over the mountains, near the seat of trouble in the Brec country, as soon as the rains ceased, that we might seek a way of deliverance for the captive children. In due time the elders and all who were interested, gathered from all the churches at the village of Sau-pe-le-cho for this new kind of warfare. During the time that elapsed from the capture of the children to that of this assembling of the Christian workers, the excitement greatly increased. It is true, said they, that God delivered His ancient people many times from their enemies; but the Karens are a poor people, and few in numbers. Perhaps He would deliver the white people, but will He take pity on us Karens? It became for them a test question of absorbing interest. At our place of meeting were assembled a great body of disciples, and two days were spent in conference and prayer.

Repeated demands were made upon Tee Peh, in the name of the great Yuah, for the deliverance of the captives, but were met by him with a curt refusal, and also with threats, if the messengers should return without the ransom. In the meetings, the burden of the prayers was that God would put His fear in the hearts of these heathen, and that the children might be so delivered that all the heathen, far and near, might be convinced that it was the living God who had appeared in behalf of the Christians.

At the close of three days, during evening worship, messengers returned with the captive children, their captors having surrendered them freely through the impelling fear of God. The full and thrilling account of this Divine interposition is given in "Soo Thah."

Heathen Women

The effect of this upon the native Christians, in strengthening their faith and inspiring their zeal, was most happy. Said one aged pastor, as the children arrived: "Behold what God has wrought for us. We never saw captives delivered before without ransom. Our Yuah has, indeed, returned to us, and wrought for us this wonderful work, as He did for His children in olden times." Such prominence had been given this affair that the whole country was aware of the contest between Tee Peh and the Christians. Many openly declared, "This is, indeed, a struggle between Tee Peh and Yuah, the God of the Christians." And so the public and free surrender of the captives was heralded as a clear and complete victory for Yuah. Indeed, the fear of the Lord fell upon the heathen generally with great power. Applications for teacher poured in from all quarters. "We want this God," said they, "who cares for His children, to be our God." Chapels and houses for teachers were erected in many villages, and captives from various towns were freely surrendered from fear of Yuah, "the God of the Christians."

The excitement throughout the tribe also was great. How far the spiritual element entered into the motives of the people in calling for teachers it would be difficult to say; but, under the wise guidance of the native pastors, many true converts to Christ were won from the heathen through the influence of this event. Within four years about thirty villages had called teachers and begun the worship of God. The self-sacrificing devotion and zeal of these native pastors was exceedingly gratifying. They could not have endured and accomplished what they did save by the aid of the Holy Spirit.

Here again, in the winning of converts and in their subsequent spiritual growth, was clearly manifested the miraculous work of the Holy Spirit. Persecution was common, and the whole atmosphere was impregnated with their old heathen thoughts and customs. To break away from these influences was no easy matter; but, in the course of time, intelligent churches, manifesting the true spirit of Christ, sprang into existence. Schools were established, and war and robbery ceased throughout the whole tribe In comparison with the whole number of the tribe, few became true disciples; but these were rare jewels in the Saviour's crown. And their influence was most marked in transforming the morals of this great body of savages.

Thus was wrought the miracle of the reformation of the Brec tribe, and the regeneration of many of its members–at the beginning a most unpromising people, hidden away in their mountain fastnesses, far from the track of civilisation and of all Christian influences, sunken in the lowest depths of savagery, at war with all good influences, completely under the sway of the god of this world. To the all-conquering Jesus be ascribed the glory!

XVI - HOW WE CAPTURED THE MYANGYOUNG PONGYI

Early in the year 1885, the English army marched from Lower Burma upon Mandalay, the capital of the Burman Empire, then ruled by King Thee Baw. When in 1878, Meng Done Meng, the most illustrious of the Burman kings, died, the glory of that empire departed forever. After several years of intrigue, Thee Baw, a man of doubtful parentage and character, an inmate of the schools of the Buddhist priests, was brought to the throne. This was accomplished by the cunning of his half-sister and her mother, the former a princess by the name of Supi-yaw-lat, whom he subsequently married. His coronation was the signal for the beginning of bloody massacres. These were committed upon the king's own relatives, including men, women, and children, who might be able to interfere with Thee Baw's hold upon the throne. These massacres were of the most cruel character, and awakened a thrill of horror throughout the civilised world.

As an example, the governor of Rangoon, a venerable Burman, highly esteemed by the common people, was caught, and his mouth filled with gunpowder, which was exploded. Others were covered with kerosene oil and burned. At the first massacre, over eighty, with their friends and relatives, were put to death; and at the second, several hundred were reported to have met a like fate.

The English lion was hereby roused to action, and this wicked king was swept from his throne, and the dynasty of the "Golden-footed Kings, Lords of the White Elephant, Children of the Sun," came to an end forever; and the Burman Empire became part of the great Indian Empire, under the beneficent rule of her Majesty, Victoria, the Empress of India.

After the capture of Thee Baw's army, the commanding general of the English army made the fatal mistake of allowing the disbanded soldiers to retain their arms. As they were without support, they immediately formed bands for the purpose of "dacoity," or robbery. They went about the country pillaging, burning, and murdering their own people as well as foreigners. The English troops, with few exceptions, had been sent from Lower Burma into the upper country at the beginning of the war, so that that province was very poorly garrisoned.

The dacoits, seeing this, entered Lower Burma and were there joined by many of their countrymen, either through fear, or the belief that the Burman king would yet drive the English out of the land. Moreover, the emissaries of the king, commissioned by him before his dethronement, aided much in inciting the people to revolt. They led them to believe that the Burman king had already been victorious over the English armies, and that soon all the Europeans would be "driven into the sea."

The chief leaders in this revolt were the Buddhist priests. Among them was one called the Myangyoung Pongyi; taking the name of the Kyoung, or priests' temple, where he lived, located on the east side of the Sittang River, in the Tenasserim Province. He was a man of large stature, great cunning, and gained great influence among the people. The Burmans are naturally a very credulous race. They much more readily believe the most improbable story than the truth; and the more marvellous the better for them. This Pongyi took advantage of this fact, and pretended to have miraculous powers. He caused a large number of charms to be made. These consisted of cabalistic signs, figures, and sacred texts from the Betagat (the Burmese sacred book), which were printed on cloth, and blessed by the Tha-tha-na-being, or Buddhist high priest at Mandalay. These charms, he declared, would render those possessing one invulnerable. The people believed this implicitly, as was afterwards shown by the reckless way in which they exposed their lives in encounters with the English soldiers.

On the 12th of December the English residents of Lower Burma were thrown into great alarm by reports that the Myangyoung Pongyi, with several thousand Shans and others, was devastating the country within less than a hundred miles of Rangoon, the largest city of Burma. Immediately, as if by magic, armed bands sprang up all over English territory. Before the close of January of that year, more than a score of towns and villages had been captured, pillaged, and wholly or in part burned. In many of these towns the police had joined the rebels, taking their arms with them. In some places the local Burmese governors also had gone over to the insurgents. Much public, as well as private, property had been destroyed. The great canals uniting the Irrawady and Sittang rivers had been broken, and thousands of teak logs set adrift to the sea.

As the days of December and January wore slowly away, the feeling of insecurity among the English, from the rulers down, increased. Like most mountaineers, the Karens are an independent and brave people. Yet up to this time they had been regarded by the English, as by their former Burman masters, as base and cowardly, because of their naturally peaceable and docile nature. On the other hand, the Burmans were regarded as the noblemen of the country. But the events now transpiring were rapidly reversing these opinions.

And now small bands of English soldiers were marching in hot haste through the country, striving to check the uprising of the people. Distracting reports filled the air. The destruction of the telegraph lines added to the general confusion.

Toungoo is an inland city about one hundred and sixty miles north of Rangoon, and had at that time a population of about twenty-four thousand Burmans. The mission "compound" is on the bank of the Sittang River, in the heart of the city. Rumours of a rising of the inhabitants of the whole city began to fill the air. Every European was armed, and the streets were patrolled night and day. The Karen Christians rallied around us for our protection. One night an attempt was made to fire the mission building, but was foiled by our Karen protectors. The missionaries were the special objects of hatred on the part of the Burmans, because of the help rendered by them in gathering news for the government through the Karen Christians.

Meanwhile, the Myangyoung Pongyi was desolating the land. However, on the 19th of December, being repulsed from the large town of Shway-gyen, on the Sittang River, he retreated with a thousand followers into the mountains to the eastward. As soon as he reached the hills, the Karens fell upon him, and greatly harassed him, impeding his progress. These Burmans, accustomed as they were to despise the Karens as weaklings, doubtless expected an easy conquest of their country. But now they were being rudely awakened to their misconception of these people, and were doomed to a still more painful surprise.

At this stage of the conflict, an appeal was made to the government by the Karens all over Lower Burman for arms for their own protection. There were then about twenty-seven thousand Christians of this race, and they were proving themselves to be the most loyal and trustworthy of all the Queen's native subjects in Burma. Moreover, they had met the rebels in several pitched battles, and had shown remarkable bravery, which had attracted the favourable notice of their rulers. Their appeal was at once acceded to, and soon the despised Karens were in high favour with the authorities, and they proved a large factor in reducing the province to order.

In the Toungoo and Shway-gyen districts there were about seven thousand of these Christian Karens, who were led by their brave native pastors. At about this time an attack was made upon a Christian Karen village, in which the chapel, schoolhouse, and most of the dwellings were utterly destroyed. The pastor of the church hastily gathered his followers and set out in pursuit of the dacoits. So sharp was the following that they were surprised in their camp before noon, and the whole band captured. That night the Karens returned to their burned village, and bound the dacoits to the charred posts of their houses for safe-keeping. In their attack upon their village the enemy declared to the Karens that their Lord Jesus was dead, and could no longer help them. Now the victorious Karen retorted, "Where is your god?"

The next day these prisoners were turned over to the nearest military station, and the Karens received the thanks of the government. This incident characterises the spirit of the Christian Karens among whom the Myangyoung Pongyi had fallen. A few days after this occurrence, another Christian village further in the mountains was surprised, while the people were at worship, and the whole congregation captured. Having possessed themselves of the chapel, a Pongyi took the pulpit, and, after ordering the Bible and other books to be cut in pieces, he proclaimed, "Jesus Christ is dead, and His worship is at an end." In this case, the Karens had taken the precaution to hide their arms the preceding night, as they would not think of fighting on the Sabbath; but on Monday morning they quietly drew them forth from their concealment, and followed the dacoits. Finding them at their evening encampment, the Karens boldly attacked them, though greatly outnumbered. The pastor and several of his flock were shot; but the dacoits suffered much, and were so terrified by the boldness of the attack that they fled in confusion.

Previous to this the main band had been vigorously attacked by these brave mountaineers, who had rallied from every village. They had also fought them with fire; for the jungles at the time were very dry and dense, and the flames burned fiercely; so that the dacoits were driven from their hiding-places and scattered. They thus found a worse foe to fight than the English soldiers on the plains.

Many of the Shans following the Myangyoung Pongyi had brought with them their wives and children. These latter, by their frequent crying, became a source of danger to them by attracting the attention of the Karens to their places of concealment. Hence, whenever a child cried, the brutal commander would order its immediate execution. In this way many children among the dacoits perished.

Soon runners from our own villages came to Toungoo, bringing reports that their towns and villages were being destroyed by the rebels. The excitement became intense, and the fear of the natives was very great; for they were as yet almost without arms for defence. We had made repeated appeals to the government to supply our people with guns and ammunition; for it was apparent that without these they would be destroyed by their implacable foes. These were at last secured, though with no little difficulty, as certain Burman officials, through their jealousy of the Karens, were striving to defeat our plans. By this time a large number of our Christian Karens had gathered on the mission compound, waiting for help. Within a half-hour from the time the arms were received they were distributed, luggage was packed on the backs of bearers, and we were off on our march to the seat of trouble among the blue hills to the eastward.

Once on the road, we had time to think of the novel position into which we had been thrust. However, we determined it should be a mission of peace and mercy as far as possible; and, indeed, we found ample opportunity for saving life, and ministering to the wounded. We freely confess, however, that we formed the purpose of capturing, if possible, the Myangyoung Pongyi. We reasoned that, now having been battered and bruised by the English troops, and subsequently by the Karens, and having been much reduced in strength for want of food, both he and his followers must be much demoralised. With this special object in view, we distributed our armed men so as to guard every path by which the rebels would seek to escape.

The second day of our march brought us into the disturbed country, and on the third we were in the heart of the trouble. And now our trials begun. We met a large band, and quickly dispersed them. Wounded men began to arrive for medical treatment. Three native Christians had been shot. A native pastor had secured a government gun and, while standing guard at one of the approaches to his village, had met a party of thirteen of the enemy, two of them with guns. The leader attempted to shoot him, but his gun missed fire. The second dacoit then attempted to shoot him, but the native pastor was too quick for him and shot him dead, at the same time putting the whole band to flight. At night prisoners began to arrive, and now we found our mission to be one of saving lives; for the Karens were so exasperated by the killing and wounding of their comrades that, for the time, their old savage instincts were likely to get control of them. Doubtless, without restraint, they would, in some instances, at least, have administered summary punishment to their prisoners.

The next morning we marched directly to the reported stronghold of the Myangyoung Pongyi. Prisoners had assured us of his position, and that he and his followers were much disheartened. Meanwhile, the Myooke, or local governor, a Karen Christian, had joined us with a small body of Karen police. We now numbered, with those guarding the villages and roads, over a hundred armed men. Reaching the rendezvous of the dacoits, we found they had left; but the dead bodies, with evidences of hasty departure, showed us that they had again been successfully attacked by the hillmen south of us. That night prisoners were brought in by scores–men, women, and some children, the latter in great distress; and again we had the privilege of saving life, and of relieving much suffering.

The next day a notable prisoner was brought in, or so his captors claimed; "for," they said "he has gold, and must, therefore, be a great man." Gold is rarely met with among these hillmen, and hence their estimate of the importance of this captive. It appeared from their account that the previous night, at one of the most distant Christian villages, a man came to some Karen women, who were husking rice by pounding it in a mortar, for their evening meal. Standing at a distance and, as he could not speak the language of the people, making motions, he indicated that he was hungry and wanted food. The women were alarmed and shook their heads. He stepped forward and held out a handful of silver; but, still fearing he was one of the dacoits, they shook their heads and retreated. The stranger then held out a handful of gold, pointing to the rice they had been cleaning.

It flashed upon them that, as he seemed to be alone, their men could capture him; and that he might be a man of importance, as he had so much wealth with him. So they nodded assent, and took him up into their house. While one of the women proceeded to cook the rice, the other went rapidly down the narrow path to call the men of the village, who were on guard, having the one government gun which had been given them. They returned, and two of them went into the house just as the stranger was sitting down on the floor to eat.

The two men succeeded in throwing the stranger off his guard, his famishing hunger doubtless helping to calm his fears. Before he had finished eating, one of the men, having worked his way behind him, took a woman's skirt; hanging near, and suddenly drew it over the head of the stranger. The whole company now set upon him, reinforced by those waiting outside, and, though fighting desperately, he was soon bound hand and foot. When brought into camp the next day, besides having his hands tied, he was led by three ropes, one around his neck, another fastened about his waist, and a third secured to his bound hands. He had made desperate attempts to escape, hence these precautions of his captors.

As soon as he was brought before the Myooke, that officer fastened his eyes upon him, and exclaimed: "Ah-Mai-gyee! You have caught the Myangyoung Pongyi himself, the leader of this rebellion! 'Tis he surely. I know him well. There is a five-thousand-rupee reward for his capture" (A rupee is equal to about thirty-five cents in our money.)

This so excited those who had suffered most at his hands, that it was difficult to restrain them from killing him then and there. The next day the march was begun towards the nearest military post. There was a long train of prisoners, besides their recent leader. On the way the latter called the Myooke, and said to him: "You are a great man, and so am I. I have gold, silver, precious stones, and elephants. Let me escape, and all these riches are yours." The Christian Myooke replied, "Were you able to give me heaven and earth, I would not let you go."

The next day the captured chief acted as if he were weak, and pleaded that his hands might be loosed while he was eating his rice. On this being granted, he watched his opportunity, and, hurling aside several of the guard, came very near escaping. But one of the guards clubbed him down with the butt of his gun. After this he was more closely watched than ever, and so he was securely brought to our mission compound, and delivered up to the proper authorities. This capture excited special excitement among the English residents throughout the country. And large numbers of the native population, as well as of the English, came to see him.

The disgust of those English officers, who had been hunting this Pongyi for months, was naturally very great. Said one, as he stood looking at the prisoners gathered in the mission compound, "Who captured these?" "These Karen Christians," was the reply. "What! these Karens? (with a slight sneer). Can they fight?" "Well, sir," was the reply, "they don't like to, but they have made this attempt." Turning to a fellow officer, he said, with supreme disgust: "See here, I have been hunting this Pongyi for three months. If I had caught him, I should have secured the five thousand rupees and a promotion; and now these Karens have got him and the reward."

This capture broke the backbone of the rebellion; for all the Burmans regarded the Myangyoung Pongyi as invincible. It also raised the despised Karen Christians to a high plane in the esteem of all good men, and of the rulers of the country. But their surprise knew no bounds, when these honest Karens brought in with their prisoners the large sums of gold and silver that had been captured with them, and laid the treasure at their feet. In reply to their expressions of astonishment, the Karen Christians said: "It is not ours. We bring it to you." Having received the reward of five thousand rupees, they first helped those who had suffered loss by the rebels, and then divided the remainder among their schools. This is how we captured the Myangyoung Pongyi.

THE END